# Guided HIGHLIGHTED Reading

## A CLOSE-READING STRATEGY FOR NAVIGATING COMPLEX TEXT

Elaine M. Weber

Barbara A. Nelson

Cynthia Lynn Schofield

*MEETS COMMON CORE STANDARDS*

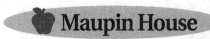

Maupin House

*Guided Highlighted Reading:*
*A Close-Reading Strategy for Navigating Complex Text*

By Elaine M. Weber, Barbara A. Nelson & Cynthia Lynn Schofield
© 2012 Maupin House Publishing, Inc.
Cover Design: Studio Montage
Book Design: Mickey Cuthbertson

Library of Congress Cataloging-in-Publication Data
Weber, Elaine M.
  Guided highlighted reading : a close-reading strategy for navigating complex text /
  by Elaine M. Weber, Barbara A. Nelson, Cynthia Lynn Schofield.
           p. cm.
      Includes bibliographical references.
      ISBN 978-1-936700-53-0 (alk. paper)
      1.  Guided reading. 2.  Reading comprehension.  I. Nelson, Barbara A., 1943- II.
      Schofield, Cynthia Lynn. III. Title.
  LB1050.377.W43 2012
  372.41'62--dc23
                        2012002741

Maupin House publishes professional resources for K-12 educators. Contact us for tailored, in-house training or to schedule an author for a workshop or conference. Visit **www.maupinhouse.com** for free lesson plan downloads.

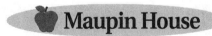

Maupin House Publishing, Inc.
2300 NW 71st Place
Gainesville, FL 32653
www.maupinhouse.com
800-524-0634
352-373-5588
352-373-5546 (fax)
info@maupinhouse.com

10 9 8 7 6 5 4 3 2

## Dedication

To Superintendent Michael DeVault, who fights fiercely for the education of all kids and the professional rights of teachers. He is my hero. –Elaine Weber

In loving memory of Harold Nelson, who knew the power of education and of educators. The search for knowledge enriches life. –Barbara Nelson

In memory of Jacqueline "Jackie" Pieper, my speech therapist, who taught me to speak through reading. Her moral compass and dedication to students provided me with an exemplary role model.
–Cynthia Schofield

# Acknowledgements

Our sincere thanks to all the teachers, literacy coaches, and administrators who have supported the strategy of guided highlighted reading (GHR) in classrooms, workshops, and schools. Thank you for sharing feedback on the success your students have experienced as a result of this strategy.

We especially want to thank Cynthia Fredenburg and Marty Zimmerman who related their experiences with GHR, and Shannon Griffin for sharing her high school data that showed the effect of GHR on students' literacy growth with formal assessment measures.

We would like to thank high school students Alina and Olivia Albrecht for the hours they spent trying out materials and giving us feedback from a student's perspective.

We want to extend our thanks to the Macomb Intermediate School District (MISD) for providing us with resources and professional environment in the development and implementation of this innovative and effective reading strategy.

# Table of Contents

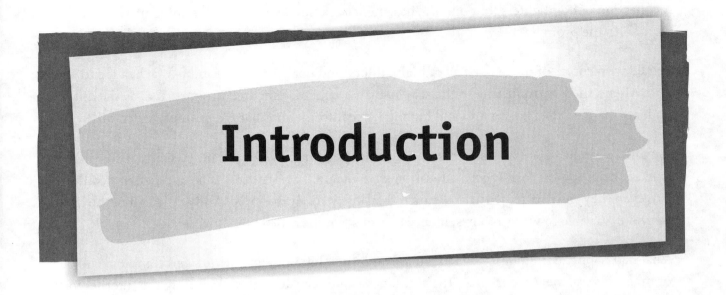

# Introduction

Like so many other creative solutions, *Guided Highlighted Reading* is a child of frustration and desperation.

Four years ago, Dr. Elaine Weber, co-author of this resource, was working as a consultant for the Macomb Intermediate School District (MISD), teaching two days' worth of close and critical reading strategies to a mixed-ability class of high school juniors and seniors.

To begin the day, she divided the class into small groups and asked the students to work together to summarize a piece of text. To her surprise and dismay, the students could not identify the salient points of the text or compose a well-written summary. In fact, it became quickly apparent that the students were not engaged in the text nor did they really comprehend it. The hour quickly ended, and Elaine realized with horror that there were still four classes and one more day to go. Even after she modified the lessons, every class that day yielded the same results.

Elaine went home and reflected on the day. She knew that she needed a text that would interest the students, and she had to find a way to hold students accountable to what they were reading. She remembered that many of the students had indicated interest in careers in the medical profession, so she found and selected a fairly difficult article written by Dr. Mehmet Oz about promising medical advances.

Next, she analyzed Dr. Oz's article to determine the points that would help students write a summary. She prepared the text by numbering the paragraphs for easy reference. Then, instead of creating questions for students to answer, Elaine wrote prompts that referred to salient points in the text. She hoped that the prompts would force the students to return to the text to find their answers.

A collection of highlighters found in the basement became the tools that the students would use to respond to the prompts.

Armed with copies of the text, a bag of highlighters, and her prepared prompts, she headed to Day Two. After a short introduction to the article, Elaine read the prepared prompts and, as she did, students scanned the texts to find and highlight the information that the prompts called for.

The difference between the first and second day was striking. Every student was engaged in the activity, including the four special education students. In fact, after students had highlighted the text, even they were surprised at how much they knew about the topic. And at the end of the lesson, everyone was able to write a four-sentence summary of the article.

What had happened? Students had exhibited an ownership in their learning and thinking, and, for many, it was a new experience. These students were accustomed to skimming the Internet for summaries and relying on teachers to tell them what a piece of text was about. They were pleased to discover they could dig into text, extract something worth discussing, and express it in a memorable form.

That day marked the beginning of the guided highlighted reading (GHR) strategy detailed in this resource. The GHR strategy that has developed from that first encounter has now experienced similar results in hundreds of workshops and classroom sessions led around the country by the authors of this book.

## Defining Guided Highlighted Reading

Simply stated, guided highlighted reading (GHR) is a text-based reading strategy that provides explicit support for the close and analytical reading of difficult and complex text in any discipline of study. Teachers choose a short complex text and prepare prompts, generally for one reading purpose at a time. They make the copies available to the students and then read each prompt aloud. Students return to the text to find the words and phrases that support their answers. The focus is on the complete text: to read and understand information that may be beyond the independent reading level of a student.

GHR is designed to be a temporary scaffold, not an end in itself. If placed on the "Gradual Release of Responsibility" chart, it would appear at the top, in the spot that shows where a task is too difficult without support of the teacher's prompts and guidance. As students acquire the skill of close and observant reading, the responsibility is released.

Research with students in Michigan demonstrates that GHR is an effective reading strategy. Because it offers all students exposure to complex texts, as well as explicit support for close and analytical reading of those texts in any discipline, it directly supports the Common Core State Standards for English Language Arts & Literacy in History/Social Studies, Science, and Technical Subjects objectives.

## What This Resource Includes

*Guided Highlighted Reading* explains this effective reading strategy for teachers in grades 4 and up. It shows you how to choose and prepare text for four key reading purposes: summary, author's craft, vocabulary, and multiple-choice test preparation. Each purpose has been carefully aligned with Common Core objectives, which are included.

The resource offers opportunities to try samples of each strategy with students for each of the reading purposes using short passages that are taken directly from Appendix B of the Common Core State Standards for English Language Arts & Literacy in History/Social Studies, Science, and Technical Subjects.

In an attempt to illustrate the versatility of GHR, we have provided different genres over a range of grade levels. These include two fourth-grade texts, a poem, and an informational text. The sixth- through eighth-grade levels include a science text, a history text, a fictional narrative, and an informational language arts text. The ninth- through tenth-grade level includes three informational language arts texts. Finally, the eleventh-grade text sample is an informational language arts text.

In addition, we have included a preview of how GHR can be applied to help students find evidence in texts. Finding evidence in texts is the first step in supporting the ability to analyze and synthesize multiple texts. That skill is expected to be part of the SMARTER Balanced Assessment Consortium (SBAC) recommendations due out in the 2014 school year.

To extend your use of the book, the model examples, rubrics, additional pieces of prepared text, and reference-text cites are prepared for each of the specific purposes. These resources appear in the Appendix at the end of the book. Potential handouts for professional development sessions are also included in this section.

Chapter Three discusses formative and summative assessment options.

Throughout the resource, sidebars from the authors provide more insight into the strategy, offer teacher in-service suggestions, and explain how GHR can be applied to various texts, grade levels, and content areas.

## GHR: An Effective Scaffold and Starting Point

As you work with GHR, you will see that this strategy can be applied to more than the four reading purposes outlined here. However you choose to use it, the result will be the same: By deliberately inviting your students to revisit complex text, they gain confidence, and their reading competency with difficult text grows.

Guided highlighted reading was born out of frustration and desperation, but it has evolved into a strategy of hope. This book was written in the hope that *Guided Highlighted Reading: A Close-Reading Strategy for Navigating Complex Text* will support teachers in their quest to help all students become skilled and competent readers of complex text.

# CHAPTER 1

# Understanding Guided Highlighted Reading

*Guided Highlighted Reading is a simple and effective text-driven strategy that scaffolds the close reading of complex informational and narrative text.*

Guided highlighted reading functions like training wheels on a bicycle. The GHR prompts function as the extra wheels that provide a feeling of safety as the reader learns how to control the balance, momentum, and direction required to accomplish a close reading of difficult text—metaphorically learning how to "ride the bicycle" by himself. GHR supports readers as they practice reading for summary, author's craft, vocabulary, and multiple-choice test preparation. At some point, the GHR scaffold will no longer be needed.

The goal of GHR is for students to experience success in summarizing, acquiring vocabulary, analyzing text for author's craft, and preparing for multiple-choice tests. If students are prompted to find the salient points of a text, they are able to write a summary. If the prompts lead them to find examples of author's craft in a text, they will be able to write an analysis of the choices that an author makes during writing. If students are prompted with appropriate synonyms, they will be able to define vocabulary in the context of the text. And, if students are prompted to return to the text to identify the patterns of questioning, they will be successful on multiple-choice tests.

## How is Guided Highlighted Reading Different?

For years, classroom teachers have assumed that if students read every day, their competency with reading skills is bound to improve. Unfortunately, reading test scores and national trends—as well as teacher observation and research—concur that this approach is not working.

Current reading strategies that teachers depend on are firmly grounded in research about the process of reading, and they have proven themselves over time. In *Developing Expertise in Reading Comprehension,* David Pearson and his colleagues noted the seven processes of proficient readers:

- Activating background knowledge to make connections between new and known information
- Questioning the text
- Drawing inferences
- Determining importance
- Creating mental images
- Repairing understanding when meaning breaks down
- Synthesizing information

Effective strategies have been developed based on these processes. The success of the strategies is dependent on all students being focused on the text. These research-based processes lack a systematic way to engage students in the text to acquire the foundational understanding of what the text says (and thus use the strategies to construct meaning from the text). GHR is the missing link.

The strategies alone do not insure that students have understood what the text says. When students face challenging and complex text, they must read in layers to capture the various aspects of the text: difficult words, text structures, figures of speech, salient points, etc. Once they have demonstrated that understanding, then they are ready to employ the strategies to construct the meaning from the text.

GHR characteristics shown below outline the missing foundational skills that insure that students are prepared to employ the reading process strategies to build and construct meaning from text.

Guided highlighted reading:

- is text-driven and meaning-based
- focuses students on the context of text
- guides students to read for one reading purpose at a time
- invites and guides students to revisit the text more than once
- guides students to return to the same text for multiple purposes
- targets the acquisition of skills needed for close and critical reading
- builds fluency and stamina in readers
- uses multiple senses: visual, auditory, and kinesthetic

Like reading-process strategies, GHR does require teachers to prepare before a lesson. However, the preparation is well worth the time because it *always* yields success. Many reading strategies do connect with a few students, but GHR gives every student the opportunity to successfully summarize the text, analyze craft, or access vocabulary. Guided highlighted reading front-loads students toward mastery of complex text.

Marty Zimmerman, a Michigan high school and middle school literacy coach, told us this story about guided highlighted reading. Bob, a veteran teacher, asked Marty for a strategy that would improve the ability of his fifth graders to read and retain information from their history textbooks. Marty asked for a copy of the text that would be used next. He developed a guided highlighted reading lesson using the chapter, "Europeans Come to the Americas," and passed out copies and highlighters for the students. The students had no prior exposure to the GHR strategy.

After the students read the text and highlighted the responses to the prompts, Marty asked them to turn their handouts facedown on their desks. The students were told to wait until he had counted to three before answering the questions he would ask them. He asked, "What are the 1400s known for?" He counted to three, and a simultaneous chorus of all voices enthusiastically sang out, "The age of discovery!"

Marty continues, "Unknown to me, Bob had positioned himself next to his three 'non-readers,' as he called them. He simply watched and observed them. Later, he told me they sometimes managed to highlight as I had prompted them, and sometimes they missed and had to skip."

But Marty said that Bob had been astonished to see them doing exactly the same thing the others were. Their eyes scanned the text just as everyone else did. "Bob told me he had not thought that behavior was possible for them," Marty said.

"As I listened to Bob, the lesson for me—especially when dealing with mixed-ability classes—is not to become obsessed with every student highlighting in reply to every prompt, thus slowing the flow down for everyone and turning momentum into drudgery."

**Barbara:** Guided highlighted reading is flexible. You, as the teaching professional, will determine the needs of your students, the purpose of the prompts, and the complex text that will support curricular goals.

Instead, Marty advises that teachers should encourage every student to do his best, knowing that the performance of the striving readers will improve over time. "Appreciate that students at their individual levels are both engaged and stretching their reading capacity and reading muscles as you repeat, 'find and highlight, find and highlight.'"

**Cynthia:** When reading *The Great Gatsby*, I can effectively guide students through the prompts to see Fitzgerald's use of color. Once students see the color motif that Gatsby employs and associates the colors with symbolism, they are unable to return to their previous blindness. In addition, they are able to take that knowledge to other texts. Recently, I was talking to a student who had discovered a science fiction author who used a color motif to expand upon the characterization.

## GHR and Complex Texts

A 2006 report published by ACT, the non-profit educational organization, supports the need to help students master difficult and complex text. In *Reading Between the Lines,* the ACT studied which reading skills separated the students who met or exceeded the benchmark score on the ACT reading section from those who did not.

Interestingly, the report noted that the reading and thinking skills of making inferences or drawing conclusions and the cognitive processes of finding the main idea, finding supporting ideas, or determining the meaning of words in context (process-based skills) *were not* what differentiated those who performed well from those who did not.

Instead, the ACT reported that the distinguishing skill of proficient readers was the *ability to answer questions about complex text.*

Future high-stakes assessments based on the Common Core State Standards (due out in 2014) will emphasize the central importance of a text-based reading approach. During a test, after all, a student quickly glances at the title, source, and author, and then is left with only the text—along with the added challenge of limited time.

**"Text complexity** – the inherent difficulty of reading and comprehending a text combined with consideration of reader and task variables; in the Standards, a three-part assessment of text difficulty that pairs qualitative and quantitative measures with reader-task considerations (CCSS, pp. 31, 57; Reading, pp. 4–16)" CCSS, ELA Appendix A, p. 43

Appendix B of the Common Core State Standards for English Language Arts illustrates the importance of complex texts by providing exemplars of reading text at every grade level. The value of this document is obvious: it provides teachers with text samples at various grade levels that would meet the criteria for complexity and quality required by the Standards.

Appendix A of the Common Core State Standards for English Language Arts makes specific reference to the *Reading Between the Lines* report and the importance of having complex text in the curriculum. The Common Core State Standards, however, modified the attributes of complexity and created a model with three components: Qualitative, Quantitative, and Reader and Task. The Standards explore these aspects in detail on pp. 2-16 of ELA Appendix A and provide a way to place texts according to grade level.

The *Reading Between the Lines* report helps us identify the definition of complex texts. It noted six aspects that contribute to increasing complexity within texts: relationships, richness, structure, style, vocabulary, and purpose (RSVP). Guided highlighted reading addresses each aspect of the complex text definition. (See the chart on p. 11; also Reproducible 1a.)

The ability to identify complex text is an essential skill and a worthy topic to explore at a staff development meeting. To see how the six aspects of complexity are applied to an exemplary text from ELA Appendix B, see Reproducible 1b.

The importance of these aspects of complexity cannot be overstated or overemphasized, and every teacher should become familiar with them. The ACT report, *Reading Between the Lines*, states that students who correctly answer questions based on complex texts can score potentially as many as 10 points higher on average than scores associated with correctly answering questions based on uncomplicated texts.

The report concludes, "...performance on complex texts is the clearest differentiator in reading between students who are likely to be ready for college and those who are not. And this is true for all genders, all racial/ethnic groups, and all family income levels."

This research has implications for classroom teachers as they prepare all students for today's complex world. Supporting students in the reading of complex texts can level the playing field; students have the potential to transcend socially constructed barriers.

**Cynthia:** The high school ELA texts recommended by the Michigan Merit Curriculum are not all noted in ELA Appendix B of the Common Core State Standards, but they certainly fit the criteria of complex texts. For example, Zora Neale Hurston's book, *Their Eyes Were Watching God*, is a complex text according to the six aspects of ACT's criteria (RSVP). In addition, the novel expands the Common Core to include another voice that deserves to be heard.

Complex texts challenge the reader. Reading complex texts requires skill to uncover opaque or obscure meaning when a reader has little practice in reading such texts. Guided highlighted reading enables students to negotiate the text by making *visible* what was previously invisible. In other words, students can clearly see—literally and metaphorically—meaning that once was murky and inaccessible.

**Cynthia:** I noticed two identical Van Gogh prints hanging on a wall with the same frames but with different mats. The two mats caused the pictures to look totally different; they literally reframed the prints. In the same way, guided highlighted reading reframes complex text. It allows the reader to understand the text with new eyes.

## Reading for Four Purposes

Reading a complex text for one purpose at a time is the basic strategy of guided highlighted reading. The four purposes described in this resource directly respond to and align with the instructional challenges posed by the Common Core State Standards for English Language Arts. These standards form a solid basis for understanding and analyzing complex texts—understanding the meaning, structure, and vocabulary of a text and analyzing it in response to a multiple-choice assessment.

### Reading for Summary

The ability to summarize is the first major building block needed to understand the meaning of complex text. The College and Career Readiness (CCR) Anchor Standards for Reading emphasize the importance of reading for literal meaning of the text. The first two Anchor Standards are concerned with key ideas and details:

CCR 1: Read closely to determine what the text says explicitly and to make logical inferences from it; cite specific textual evidence when writing or speaking to support conclusions drawn from the text.

CCR 2: Determine central ideas . . . summarize the key supporting details and ideas.

## Reading for Author's Craft

Initially, we used GHR to help students determine what was important in a piece of text in order to create a clear summary. Over time, we found that many students struggled to answer the question, "How does the author say it?" It became apparent that many students were unaware of the effect that an author's craft and structural decisions had on a reader's understanding of the text. Typically, students had no language to describe these craft decisions if they did perceive them.

In addition, students often did not return to a difficult text for a second read, which is a necessary strategy when they are confronted with complex text. This led us to analyze a text selection for genre, structure, purpose, tone, figurative language, argument, bias, privilege, etc.

A second round of prompts that used the same passages was then created to guide students to return to the text to identify the author's craft. The second time through the text, students read for craft and structure.

The College and Career Readiness Anchor Standards for Reading support analyzing text for author's craft and structure.

CCR3: Analyze how and why individuals, events, and ideas develop and interact over the course of a text.

CCR 4: Interpret words and phrases as they are used in a text, including determining technical, connotative, and figurative meanings, and analyze how specific word choices shape meaning or tone.

CCR 5: Analyze the structure of texts, including how specific sentences, paragraphs, and larger portions of the text (e.g., a section, chapter, scene, or stanza) relate to each other and the whole.

CCR 6: Assess how point of view or purpose shapes the content and style of a text.

The College and Career Readiness Anchor Standards for Language also support analyzing text for author's craft including figurative language. The fifth anchor standard for K-12 and 6-12 is as follows:

CCR 5: Demonstrate understanding of word relationships and nuances in word meanings.

**Reading for Vocabulary Acquisition**

As we continued to work with GHR, we realized that summary and author's craft were not the only reading purposes that would scaffold students to understanding difficult and complex text. A lack of sufficient vocabulary stood in the way, too, so we explored the possibilities of expanding GHR to include it.

We discovered that Tier II academic vocabulary words made complex text difficult. Unlike Tier III (domain-specific vocabulary,) Tier II words are rarely defined in context or developed in pre-reading activities. Scaffolding new Tier II words provided students with the greatest amount of comprehension support (see Common Core State Standards, ELA Appendix A, p. 33).

The College and Career Readiness Anchor Standards 4, 5, and 6 for Language all involve vocabulary acquisition and use:

> CCR 4: Determine or clarify the meaning of unknown and multiple-meaning words and phrases by using context clues, analyzing meaningful word parts, and consulting general and specialized reference materials, as appropriate.

> CCR 5: Demonstrate understanding of figurative language, word relationships, and nuances in word meanings.

> CCR 6: Acquire and use accurately a range of general academic and domain-specific words and phrases sufficient for reading, writing, speaking, and listening at the college and career readiness level; demonstrate independence in gathering vocabulary knowledge when considering a word or phrase important to comprehension or expression.

**Reading for Multiple-Choice Test Preparation**

High-stakes assessments of reading comprehension in many states include multiple-choice questions that determine how well students can read and comprehend complex text. For instructional purposes, multiple-choice tests feature patterns and predictable categories so that they actually resemble a genre. GHR enables students to recognize these patterns, while at the same time making clear the most salient content.

Multiple-choice questions are commonly used to assess comprehension of content and processes across disciplines. The content and/or process typically include knowledge of vocabulary, theme, thesis or purpose, supporting details, text structure, genre, etc.

To be successful with multiple-choice assessments, students have to read for multiple purposes at the same time, and often the process is timed. Although students may be trained in the test-taking skills required for multiple-choice assessments, the complexity of texts to read and analyze in a timed situation is ignored or not explicitly taught until it is too late—when high school students are faced with the timed multiple-choice assessments of the ACT and SAT.

Michigan students are required to take the ACT assessment as part of high school graduation requirements; at the time of publication, at least five other states require all high school juniors to take the ACT: Illinois, Kentucky, Tennessee, Wyoming, and Colorado.

Macomb County teachers had been using the GHR strategy to support students who struggled with text as well as better readers who were challenged by complex text. Thus, it seemed logical to use it to prepare Michigan students for the ACT reading assessment, too.

In 2009, high school students at New Haven Community Schools participated in a study to see the effect of guided highlighted reading (GHR) on the performance of students on ACT reading passages in different content areas. GHR prompts were prepared for sample ACT passages in each of four areas: prose fiction, social science, humanities, and natural science.

In the fall of 2009, juniors and all other students who would be taking the ACT test the following spring were given a practice ACT assessment. Over the school year, approximately one hundred students had eleven to thirteen practices with GHR passages, along with ten multiple-choice, ACT-like questions.

Data showed that struggling students benefitted the most from GHR intervention. This group of students averaged two additional points on the actual ACT reading portion of the assessment, a statistically significant amount. That same school year, other high schools in Macomb County provided similar interventions, and, although they were not formally part of the study, they too indicated improved ACT reading scores.

Research reported by Fitzgerald Public Schools in Warren, Michigan, showed positive results on multiple-choice tests with GHR as well. Assistant Superintendent for Curriculum Shannon Griffin initially introduced guided highlighted reading at Fitzgerald High School as an intensive, two-month intervention. Core and non-core areas were asked to use specific course-related readings twice weekly, while ELA courses used them as many as four times a week.

The intervention resulted in significant gains on the ACT portion of the Michigan Merit Exam 2010. The MME reading score alone increased thirteen percentage points (from 36 percent to 49 percent). The State of Michigan averaged an increase of five percentage points. In 2010, the ACT Reading score increased from 15.9 in 2009 to 17.2 (1.3 point increase, or about 8 percent), while the state average ACT reading score increased from 19.7 to 20.1 (.4 point increase, or about 2 percent).

Even though the Fitzgerald scores were below the state average, all other content area tests increased during the spring 2010 test at a rate higher than the state in each content area. This resulted in the district's ACT composite score increasing a full percentage point (16.0 to 17.0), or 6 percent. The State's composite score increased from 19.7 to 20.0 during the same time period—or 1.5 percent.

**Cynthia:** The difficult texts that I read awaken me to new thinking. Apply RSVP to your own reading, too. When I bring the book I am reading to class and share my excitement, it opens a dialogue. The students see me struggle, and the struggle becomes part of the journey. In today's find-it-quick world, this is no small accomplishment.

## GHR and the ACT's Six Elements of Complex Text

**Richness:** The text possesses a sizable amount of highly sophisticated information conveyed through data or literary devices.

**Guided Highlighted Reading for Summary and Craft**

**Relationships:** Interactions among ideas or characters in the text are subtle, involved, or deeply embedded.

**Guided Highlighted Reading for Summary and Craft**

**Style:** The author's tone and use of language is often intricate.

**Guided Highlighted Reading for Craft**

**Structure:** The text is organized in a way that is elaborate and sometimes unconventional.

**Guided Highlighted Reading for Craft**

## Complex Text

**Vocabulary:** The author's choice of words is demanding and highly context-dependent.

**Guided Highlighted Reading for Vocabulary**

**Purpose:** The author's intent in writing the text is implicit and sometimes ambiguous.

**Guided Highlighted Reading for Craft**

# CHAPTER 2

# Using Guided Highlighted Reading to Navigate Complex Texts for Four Purposes

*"Close reading means not only reading and understanding the meanings of the individual printed words but also making the reader sensitive to all the nuances and connotations of language as it is used by writers. Close reading can focus on a wide range of issues, including discerning a word's particular meaning or the syntactic construction of a sentence, to thematic progression, author's craft, or a view of the world that a text might offer. It involves almost everything, from the smallest linguistic items to the largest issues of literacy understanding and judgment."* —Danielle S. McNamara (2007)

Complex texts require rereading. But in a contemporary society that honors immediacy in everything from fast food to the speed of an Internet connection, it is no minor feat to achieve close reading of text—not to mention rereading it—in a classroom. GHR offers teachers an effective strategy that helps their students process complex text for many specific purposes and mine for meaning in different ways. This flexible and engaging scaffolding tool enables students at all levels to respond to and comprehend complex texts.

Note that the critical concept of "purpose" is at the heart of GHR. GHR empowers teachers to explicitly guide students to explore text for specific purposes that lead to deeper comprehension.

# General Directions for the GHR Strategy

GHR is easy for students, and they will quickly learn what is expected. First, you will choose the complex text and determine which purpose you want the students to practice. You prepare the text by numbering the paragraphs or lines in the text, or the stanzas or lines in a poem.

You then write text-based prompts that relate to the reading purpose. Prompts, instead of questions, make GHR unique and effective. Remember that questions assume the information is known; prompts guide the reader to find the information. (See Reproducible 2a, "Preparing Text for Four Different Purposes.")

**GHR Checklist:**
1. Select text
2. Determine purpose
3. Number the paragraphs or lines
4. Write prompts

In some schools, the same copy of the text will be used to explore all four purposes; in that case, students can use different colored highlighters for each purpose, or they can combine underlining and circling text with highlighting for each successive purpose.

If you are reading for summary, you might want to write a short summary first to help you frame the prompts easily. Determine what essential points should appear in the summary, and write prompts to guide students to highlight the crucial elements. A prompt for summary may look like:

*In paragraph three, find and highlight the effects of a tornado.*
or
*In paragraph one, find and highlight the thesis statement.*
or
*In paragraph two, find and highlight a concept that supports the author's argument.*

If the students will be reading for author's craft, you will first analyze the text for elements of craft such as genre, organization, text features, point of view, mood, tone, figures of speech, and writing techniques like word choice. Here, you again might want to use the information gained in your analysis to write a paragraph answering the question, "How does the author say it?" to help you frame the craft prompts more easily. For example, craft prompts might include:

*In paragraph one, find and highlight the question the author uses to pull his reader into the essay.*
or
*In paragraph three, find and highlight the metaphor.*
or
*In paragraph two, find and highlight the signal word that suggests a cause-and-effect structure.*

If there are only a few potentially troublesome words, they could be addressed in summary or craft prompts. Tier II academic vocabulary words in a passage are rarely defined in context and thus need to be addressed before the student can do the close reading. In this case, you can identify the words, find content-appropriate synonyms or short definitions, and build prompts. For example,

*In paragraph one, find and highlight the word that means _____.*
or
*In paragraph three, find and highlight the word that fits the definition of _____.*

When students read to respond to multiple-choice questions, analyze the questions to determine how you can prompt students to find the answers in the text. For example,

*In paragraph one, find and highlight another name for _____.*
or
*In paragraph three, find and highlight the three things a visitor would find on _____.*
or
*In paragraph two, find and highlight the topic of the paragraph.*

## Introducing the Text and Discussing It

To prepare for GHR, give each student or group of students a copy of the text along with a highlighter pen. Consider the needs of your students and modify accordingly. For example, if the text is part of an existing unit or chapter and background has been established, have the students do a fly-over of the text, skimming for length of text, text features, topic of text, etc.

If the text is a new topic and outside of the context of what is being studied, supply the necessary background knowledge. If you think that the students may not be able to read the text themselves without difficulty, read the text aloud to them as they read along before administering the prompts. You could also read one paragraph at a time and immediately prompt for the information to be highlighted. Again, your knowledge of your class and their needs come into play here.

When you read the prompts, students are encouraged to reread the text. At first, you will read the prompts fairly slowly; after multiple practices, you'll pick up the pace to build reading fluency and prepare students for time-limited multiple-choice assessments. Keep moving through the prompts. Don't slow down to the speed of your slowest student.

You can discuss the responses with students as a class, ask students to discuss them in small groups, or simply provide the desired responses, depending on the time you have available.

The prompts can be assessed informally or formally. We suggest several different ways to assess responses in Chapter 3.

**Elaine:** Recently, a group of literacy coaches was discussing how they had made modifications when preparing prompts for GHR. Initially, they prompted for far too much information. They decided the "Goldilocks" rules should be applied—"just the right amount for the designated purpose."

## Reading to Summarize Text

All too often, teachers decide to shortcut the sometimes agonizing process of summarizing by providing the summary as a starting point. After all, time is limited, and a teacher-provided summary ensures that all students are starting from the same place. However, the cost of this convenience is too high. Summary, the first building block of comprehension, is an essential skill that students must work through for themselves.

Effective summarizing leads to an increase in student learning. Helping students recognize how information is structured will help them summarize what they read or hear. For example, summarizing of a reading assignment can be more effective when done within summary frames, which typically include a series of questions the teachers provides to direct student attention to specific content. (Marzano, R. J., Pickering, D.J., & Pollock, J.E. (2001)

Although many reading strategies can scaffold a student to comprehension, finding one that successfully connects the entire class at the same time to one text can be difficult. Because GHR requires students to study the text itself, this strategy is particularly effective in accomplishing that sometimes elusive objective quickly and effectively. As students attend to the task at hand for multiple practice readings, they will find it impossible to text or talk and still respond to prompts given at a pace that models an ever-increasing approximation of fluency.

**Directions for Using GHR for Summary**

Write a short summary to help frame the prompts easily. Prepare prompts that will scaffold students to be able to:

- Restate in their own words what the text says explicitly
- Make logical inferences
- Cite specific textual evidence to support conclusions drawn from the text
- Determine central ideas
- Summarize the key supporting details and ideas

## ELA Standards, History/Social Studies (Grades 11-12)

1. Cite specific textual evidence to support analysis of primary and secondary sources, connecting insights gained from specific details to an understanding of the text as a whole.

2. Determine the central ideas or information of a primary or secondary source; provide an accurate summary that makes clear the relationships among the key details and ideas.

## Model Text for Summary

The following model text is an excerpt from Thomas Paine's *Common Sense*. See ELA Appendix B of the Common Core State Standards, p. 164, for another Paine excerpt, and see Reproducibles 3a-f for the student-prepared text of this passage with prompts for vocabulary, summary, author's craft, and multiple-choice questions & answers.

1  The infant state of the Colonies, as it is called, so far from being against, is an argument in
2  favour of independence. We are sufficiently numerous, and were we more so we might
3  be less united. 'Tis a matter worthy of observation that the more a country is peopled, the
4  smaller their armies are. In military numbers, the ancients far exceeded the moderns; and
5  the reason is evident, for trade being the consequence of population, men became too
6  much absorbed thereby to attend to anything else. Commerce diminishes the spirit both
7  of patriotism and military defence.  And history sufficiently informs us that the bravest
8  achievements were always accomplished in the non-age of a nation. With the increase of
9  commerce England hath lost its spirit. The city of London, notwithstanding its numbers,
10  submits to continued insults with the patience of a coward. The more men have to lose,
11  the less willing are they to venture. The rich are in general slaves to fear, and submit to
12  courtly power with the trembling duplicity of a spaniel.

## Read the following prompts while students highlight as directed:

- In line #2, find and highlight what the Colonies are ready for, according to the text. (Answer: *independence*)

- In line #3, find and highlight what "we" would be if we were more numerous. (Answer: *less united*)

- In line #4, find and highlight what happens to armies when the number of people increases. (Answer: *smaller*)

- In lines #5, find and highlight the consequence of population growth. (Answer: *trade*)

- In line #6, find and highlight another word for "trade." (Answer: *commerce*)

- In lines #6-7, find and highlight what commerce diminishes. (Answer: ". . . the spirit both of patriotism and military defence.")

- In line #11, find and highlight what happens when men have more to lose. (Answer: ". . . the less willing they are to venture.")

- In line #11, find and highlight what, in general, the rich are. (Answer: ". . . slaves to fear.")

**Sample summary:**

The Colonies are ready for independence because of their newness and small numbers. Historically, countries that are numerous in population and commerce have small armies. Once countries engage in commerce they lose the will to fight. England is an example of a wealthy country that fears losing its trade and consequently tolerates abuse.

Many contemporary students do not live in the world of paper books; they were teethed on laptops. However, reading is reading, whether the words appear in a print book or in an online article. With just a few simple modifications to the print-text directions, GHR can be used to summarize online text.

**Sample of How to Use Online Text for Summary**

Adapt the directions for reading online summaries. Have students:

> Students can easily respond to the teacher's prompts via their Kindle, Nook, or iPad. The summary skill is as crucial for today's plugged-in students as it was for past print-based readers.

1. Go to the Daily Beast website to find Anna Quindlen's article, "A Quilt of a Country" (**www.thedailybeast.com/newsweek/2001/09/27/a-quilt-of-a-country.html**).

2. Copy the text in a word document

3. Number the paragraphs or lines

4. Name and save the document

5. Use the highlighting feature/command to respond to the prompts

6. Optional: Save the document in Word and mail to the teacher's email, or print out.

Require students to copy and save their Word documents to make sure they are attending to the text at hand. (See Reproducible 4b for summary prompts for the last paragraph of Anna Quindlen's article, "A Quilt of a Country," which is referenced on p. 129 of the Common Core State Standards, ELA Appendix B.)

# Reading to Analyze Text for Author's Craft

Promoting initial comprehension through summary is the main focus of the first reading of a complex text. A second close reading of the same text for a different purpose allows readers to mine or probe the text for the craft and structural decisions that affect comprehension. Students analyze the choices that an author makes to convey meaning through genre, organization, text features, point of view, mood, tone, figures of speech, writing techniques, etc.

> **Elaine:** Providing a sample summary or a description of author's craft that meets the rubric's expectations is another form of scaffolding. I call this the Martha Stewart approach, because she always begins with the completed project and works backwards to show how it was created.

The ability to discern the intentionality of author's craft is an important component of discovering meaning in text. It influences the quality of written response as well. Students who are unable to recognize intentional craft decisions lose out on the opportunity to practice reading from a writer's point of view.

The prompts awaken students to choices that might otherwise remain unnoticed. At the end of the GHR for author's craft, students should be able to answer the question "How does the author say it?" By literally making the author's craft visible, GHR maximizes the reciprocal value of writing to the reading experience.

It is important to note that author's craft exists in both informational and narrative texts. Too often, teachers consider author's craft to lie solely in the realm of fiction and poetry. In contrast, ELA Appendix B of the Common Core State Standards beautifully illustrates the wealth of craft that all well-written complex texts incorporate. Because the Common Core State Standards hold teachers of all subjects responsible for the reading of craft, guided highlighted reading for this purpose provides an easy and effective technique for non-ELA teachers, too. See Reproducible 5a-b for two charts that will scaffold students as they mine informational or narrative text for examples of author's craft. The charts can also be used to develop GHR prompts for craft.

> **Barbara:** In a recent working session with high school teachers preparing GHR experiences for the new school year, I observed teachers making good use of the charts as they created model GHR experiences for craft. One teacher who had had more experience as a history teacher found the charts particularly helpful.

**Directions for Using GHR to Analyze Text for Author's Craft**

Follow the general directions for GHR previously noted. Because author's craft comprises many different elements, you will save time in the long run if you create a teacher model that serves as a frame to compose your prompts. A sample text (the Preamble of the United States Constitution) with suggested grade levels, prompts, and the appropriate standards is provided below. You will also find this text in the Appendix prepared for student handout and use for all four reading purposes (see Reproducibles 6a-f).

**ELA Standards, Reading: Informational Text (Grades 6-8)\***

3. Analyze how a text makes connections among and distinctions between individuals, ideas, or events (e.g., through comparisons, analogies, or categories).

4. Determine the meaning of words and phrases as they are used in a text, including figurative, connotative, and technical meanings; analyze the impact of specific word choices on meaning and tone, including analogies or allusions to other texts.

5. Analyze in detail the structure of a specific paragraph in a text, including the role of particular sentences in developing and refining a key concept.

6. Determine an author's point of view or purpose in a text and analyze how the author acknowledges and responds to conflicting evidence or viewpoints.

10. By the end of the year, read and comprehend literary nonfiction at the high end of the grades 6–8 text complexity band independently and proficiently.

*\*8th Grade Standards are cited above*

**Model Text for Author's Craft**

The following model text is the Preamble of the United States Constitution. See ELA Appendix B of the Common Core State Standards, p. 93, and see Reproducible 6a-f for the student-prepared text of this passage with prompts for vocabulary, summary, author's craft, and multiple-choice questions & answers.

1    *We, the People of the United States, in Order to form a more perfect Union, establish Justice,*

2    *insure domestic Tranquility, provide for the common defense, promote the general Welfare,*

3    *and secure the Blessings of Liberty to ourselves and our Posterity, do ordain and establish*

4    *this Constitution for the United States of America.*

**Read the following prompts while students highlight as directed:**

- In the title, find and highlight the word in the heading that is a more formal word for introduction. (Answer: *Preamble*)

- In the title, find and highlight the word that means a legal document. (Answer: *Constitution*)

- In line #1, find and highlight the thesis or purpose of this document. (Answer: "... to form a more perfect Union...")

- In line #1, find and highlight the phrase that identifies "We." (Answer: "...the People of the United States...")

- In line #2, find and highlight an archaic word for harmony. (Answer: *Tranquility*)

- In lines #1-4, find and highlight the punctuation mark that ends the first sentence. (Answer: after the last word, *America*)

- When an author gives human characteristics to inanimate objects, it is called personification. In line #3, find and highlight an example of personification that tells what Liberty bestows or gives. (Answer: *blessings*)

- In lines #1-4, find and highlight the various strong verbs in present tense the authors used to indicate the benefits of the constitution. (Answer: "form," "establish," "insure," "provide," "promote," "secure," "ordain," "establish")

- The text structure of the Preamble is cause and effect, so find and highlight the effect or result. (Answer: "... a more perfect union")

**Sample analysis of author's craft:** The text is a **legal document** that states the **purpose** for its existence in the **Preamble**, or introduction. The text structure is cause and effect; the cause is the need to create a Union, and the effect is the creation of a constitution. The authors' language is academic and archaic e.g., "posterity" and "ordain." The authors use repetition to emphasize key points, for example, the phrase, "United States." Consequently, the reader is left with the impression that the United States is important enough that it bears repeating. The authors also use **capitalization** to emphasize key reasons for the existence of the Constitution, e.g. "Tranquility." The **point of view** is "We the People." It is difficult to know **who is left out** except one can assume anyone who is not considered "People of the United States." It is interesting to note that it is one **sentence** in length. The authors use numerous **commas**, but only one period, as all thoughts are interrelated. In addition, the authors use **powerful action verbs** such as "ordain" and "establish." The document is written in **present tense**, which makes the reader engage in the document as if it were now. The Preamble uses persuasive tactics; it promises that the establishment of a constitution will yield a "more perfect Union."

# Reading for Vocabulary Acquisition

Vocabulary is the great divider: It separates the academically successful student from those who do not have the words they need. While teaching a lesson, most teachers have experienced the feeling that they are speaking a foreign language as students raise their hands to ask, "What does that mean?"

Teachers often find it tempting to restrict vocabulary when speaking, just to save time. Yet, if a teacher yields to the temptation and speaks in only the simplest of words, a valuable opportunity for language acquisition is lost. A teacher must be purposeful in his/her language or word choice, and class dialogue can reinforce vocabulary acquisition.

Vocabulary has the potential to scale the walls that separate students from comprehension. GHR provides an explicit strategy to teach vocabulary acquisition in context to enhance comprehension.

> "...research shows that if students are truly to understand what they read, they must grasp upward of 95 percent of the words." – Betts, E.A. (1946); Hu Hsueh-chao, Marcella, and Paul Nation (2000); Laufer, Batia (1988)

> "When we read, it is through words that we build, refine, and modify our knowledge. What makes vocabulary valuable and important is not the words themselves so much as the understandings they afford." – Adams, Marilyn Jager (2009, p. 180)

**ELA Appendix A**

GHR supports the Common Core emphasis on the importance of vocabulary acquisition to read difficult and complex texts. Appendix A in the Common Core State Standards for English Language Arts notes three tiers of vocabulary words:

- Tier One: words of everyday speech, often found in simple narratives.
- Tier Two: "general academic" words. Vocabulary words in this tier cross disciplines and support academic learning.
- Tier Three: "domain-specific words" specific to a particular content or discipline.

*Guided Highlighted Reading* focuses on Tier Two vocabulary words because knowledge of these words wields such an enormous, positive impact on academic success in all content-area disciplines.

Despite their profound influence on learning, Tier Two words are seldom mentioned in class. Instead, time is spent on Tier Three words because they are content-specific and are often bolded in texts. Yet, it is the Tier Two words that serve as a barrier to student learning and comprehension of difficult or complex texts. Guided highlighted reading emphasizes vocabulary through explicit classroom instruction for the benefit of all students.

## Directions for Using GHR for Vocabulary Acquisition

Follow the general procedure as listed at the beginning of this chapter (p. 14). In addition, students should first skim the passage and underline the words they do not know. After the students respond to the prompts and share their responses, ask them if they still have underlined words that were not highlighted. You can ask students to define those words aloud or just define the words yourself.

Difficult vocabulary makes difficult text even more challenging to read; returning to the text to decipher unknown words increases comprehension. In the sample paragraph below from "Washington's Farewell Address," the general academic words of Tier Two are difficult for students because these words are not defined in context.

For more information about general academic vocabulary, see ELA Appendix A, pp. 33-34 of the Common Core State Standards.

## Model Text for Vocabulary Acquisition

The following model text is an excerpt of "Washington's Farewell Address" (see ELA Appendix B, p. 123, and see Reproducibles 7a-f for the student-prepared text of this passage with prompts for vocabulary, summary, author's craft, and multiple-choice questions & answers.)

1     Against the insidious wiles of foreign influence (I conjure you to believe me, fellow-

2     citizens) the jealousy of a free people ought to be constantly awake, since history and

3     experience prove that foreign influence is one of the most baneful foes of republican

4     government. But that jealousy to be useful must be impartial; else it becomes the

5     instrument of the very influence to be avoided, instead of a defense against it. Excessive

6     partiality for one foreign nation and excessive dislike of another cause those whom they

7     actuate to see danger only on one side, and serve to veil and even second the arts of

8     influence on the other. Real patriots who may resist the intrigues of the favorite are liable

9     to become suspected and odious, while its tools and dupes usurp the applause and

10    confidence of the people, to surrender their interest.

**Read the following prompts as students highlight as directed:**

- In line #1, find and highlight the phrase (two words) that means "deceptive tricks." (Answer: *insidious wiles*)

- In line #1, find and highlight the word that means *summon*. (Answer: *conjure*)

- In line #2, find and highlight the word that we usually think of as meaning envy, but also means *watchfulness*. (Answer: *jealousy*)

- In line #3, find and highlight the phrase that means evil opponents. (Answer: *baneful foes*)

- In line #4, find and highlight the word that means *neutral, independent,* and *objective.* (Answer: *impartial*)

- In line #6, find and highlight the word that means *favoritism*. (Answer: *partiality*)

- In line #7, find and highlight the word that means "to move to action." (Answer: *actuate*)

- In line #8, find and highlight the word that means *conspiracies*. (Answer: *intrigues*)

- In line #8, find and highlight the word that means "legally responsible." (Answer: *liable*)

- In line #9, find and highlight the word that means *hateful*. (Answer: *odious*)

- In line #9, find and highlight the word that means *fools*. (Answer: *dupes*)

- In line #9, find and highlight the word that means "to seize and hold." (Answer: *usurp*)

**Barbara:** As I worked with Alina, a tenth grader, on this selection, I understood what a hindrance vocabulary can be to understanding. I should have done GHR for vocabulary before we did summary because she assumed that *jealousy* meant envy and that did not make sense to her. As she did the Cloze procedure activity (see Reproducible 7b2), she said out loud, "'Now it all makes sense!'"

## Reading for Multiple-Choice Questions

Though the concept is seldom discussed, test-taking is, in itself, a type of genre. The tests connected with high stakes for schools, teachers, and students often are in a predictable multiple-choice format. Teachers feel compelled to use more time than they would like to prepare students to take tests.

Test preparation as it is typically practiced today is isolated from content and can actually hinder real learning. A teacher who spends the majority of the day preparing for a multiple-choice test shortchanges students by denying them the opportunity to explore complex material as a part of the preparation process.

A superficial reading of a text simply to answer questions in a timed setting may prepare students for a single standardized test, but it falls short of giving them the analytical tools that would prepare them to read any complex text they encounter.

The Common Core State Standard's heavy emphasis on literacy comprehension and complex texts across the disciplines gives teachers an opportunity to weave meaningful test preparation into the curriculum in a way that enhances learning. Careful review of the Standards at the various grade levels provides insight into potential assessment questions.

### ELA Standards, Reading: Informational Text (Grade 4-5)

**Fourth grade:**

1. Refer to details and examples in a text when explaining what the text says explicitly and when drawing inferences from the text.

2. Determine the main idea of a text and explain how it is supported by key details; summarize the text.

**Fifth grade:**

1. Quote accurately from a text when explaining what the text says explicitly and when drawing inferences from the text.

2. Determine two or more main ideas of a text and explain how they are supported by key details; summarize the text.

### Directions for Using GHR for Multiple-Choice Questions

The procedure for preparing prompts for multiple-choice test practice varies. If the multiple-choice questions are already created for ACT practice texts, for example, you will want to examine the questions to determine the types of prompts that will scaffold students to success.

If you need to create multiple-choice questions for a text, your questions should reflect the depth of thinking that students are capable of achieving. Depending on the purpose of the activity, students could read the multiple-choice questions prior to the GHR of the text.

Teachers need to be reflective and purposeful when developing their prompts. For example, GHR prompts for informational texts can scaffold students to success on both literal and inferential multiple-choice questions. Prompts can guide students to note main ideas, details, examples, facts, claims, arguments, evidence, and topics. Scaffolding improves how well students understand a difficult text and ensures that all students have an opportunity to experience that success. After all, the ultimate goal is the independent reading of complex texts.

**Cynthia:** Recently, after a GHR for vocabulary, one of my students was extremely pleased with his ability to answer a question regarding the tone of a piece. His knowledge of the vocabulary and consequential nuances of the word enabled him to rule out the incorrect answers.

**Model Text for Multiple-Choice Questions**

NASA's Mars Exploration Program website includes an exemplary text noted in the Common Core State Standards, ELA Appendix B: "All About Mars" (**www.mars.jpl.nasa.gov/allaboutmars/ extreme**). The site enriches the recommended text, Melvin Berger's *Discovering Mars: The Amazing Story of the Red Planet*, found in ELA Appendix B, p. 70.

To create multiple-choice questions, the teacher would follow the general directions of GHR for online texts, but pay particular attention to the reading standards of the grade level before creating the prompts and the multiple-choice questions. (See Reproducibles 8a-d for the student-prepared text of this passage with prompts for summary, author's craft, and multiple-choice questions & answers.)

**Directions to give to students:** Ask students to go to the Mars Exploration Program's webpage, "All About Mars": **http://mars.jpl.nasa.gov/allaboutmars/extreme**. Make sure that they are on the "Summary" tab. They should then copy and paste the title and the first paragraph into a word document, name the document, save it, and number the five sentences 1-5.

Using the highlighter tool in a word processing program, they can highlight the words and phrases from your prompts. Students should only highlight in the title and the first paragraph.

**Read the following prompts while students highlight as directed:**

- In the title, find and highlight the topic of the paragraph. (Answer: *Mars*)

- In the title, find and highlight the description of Mars. (Answer: *Extreme Planet*)

- In sentence #3, find and highlight the word the author uses to describe Mars as dry and lifeless. (Answer: *arid*)

- In sentence #3, find and highlight another name for Mars. (Answer: *Red Planet*)

- In sentence #3, find and highlight the phrase the author uses to describe Mars as an unfriendly place. (Answer: ". . . offers few hospitalities.")

- In sentence #5, find and highlight the three things that a visitor would find on Mars. (Answer: ". . . the largest volcano in the solar system, the deepest canyon and crazy weather and temperature patterns.")

- In sentence #5, find and highlight the name the author gives to Mars. (Answer: ". . . the ultimate lonely planet . . . ")

If you so choose, students can read the multiple-choice questions prior to the GHR prompts. The directions for the students are given below. See the Appendix, p. 93, for a reproducible set of directions.

**Multiple-choice GHR sample:**

Go to the Mars Exploration Program's webpage, "All About Mars": **http://mars.jpl.nasa.gov/ allaboutmars/extreme**. Make sure that you are on the "Summary" tab. Reread the text. Choose the *best* answer for each of the questions.

1. What is the main idea of this paragraph?
   A. Mars has the biggest volcano
   B. Mars is an extreme planet*
   C. Mars is rocky and cold
   D. Mars has the deepest canyon

2. What does the word "arid" mean in the first line?
   A. rocky
   B. crazy
   C. cold
   D. dry *

3. What words does the author use to describe Mars as unfriendly?
   A. "...offers few hospitalities." *
   B. "Fans of extreme sports..."
   C. "...the deepest canyon..."
   D. "...the Red Planet..."

4. According to this paragraph what would a visitor find on Mars?
   A. "...crazy weather and temperature patterns."
   B. "...the largest volcano..."
   C. "...the deepest canyon..."
   D. All of the above *

5. According to the author, what are three words that describe Mars?
   A. lonely, extreme, dark
   B. red, deepest, crazy
   C. extreme, red, lonely *
   D. largest, warmest, farthest

> An asterisk indicates the correct answer.

# Reading for a Combination of Purposes

### Analyzing Multiple Texts

Once teachers assess the needs of their students, they can combine (or mix and match) the four purposes of GHR using a single passage. However, the texts themselves may dictate the strategies that teachers choose to implement. For example, a poem by Emily Dickinson may require a GHR for summary and author's craft but not require one for vocabulary.

As the teaching professional, you determine the call, paying attention to the text to determine the prompts that best scaffolds your students to an understanding of the complex text. Yet, the attention and effort does not end with the teacher. GHR also requires that students pay attention to the text and hopefully begin to *value* the possibilities within their grasp.

### Preparing for CCSS Assessment

**Elaine:** The Common Core State Standards Assessments have challenged us to take GHR to a higher more complex level—helping students find the relevant relationships and connections across texts toward one big idea or theme.

Two multi-state consortia are developing a system for assessing the Common Core State Standards for English Language Arts. Both the SMARTER Balanced Assessment Consortium (SBAC) and Partnership for Assessment of Readiness for College and Careers (PARCC) Consortium are developing assessment systems that will be implemented in the school year 2014-2015.

The four purposes of GHR previously presented will support students' acquisition of specific concepts, facts, and skills. Through GHR and gradual release, students will be able to navigate complex text and answer questions that require close reading. However, the assessments being developed by SMARTER Balanced and PARCC will require more of students than just answering questions like, "what does the text say?" or "how does the author say it?"

The PARCC Model Content Frameworks for ELA-Literacy will expect students to read and comprehend complex text from a wide range of domains and assess vocabulary in the context of the reading passage. The test will assess close, analytic reading and comparing and synthesizing ideas across texts.

The SMARTER Balanced Assessment will also include multiple texts and expect students to be able to analyze and synthesize them. Students must support their analysis or "claim" with specific "evidence" from the text. In other words, students will be answering the question: "What does it mean?" This type of question requires close reading and critical reading. It extends thinking beyond the text, but it begins with text-based support.

The process of setting content specifications for this SBAC assessment system includes defining assessment claims and an acceptable level of relevant and sufficient evidence, as well as assessment targets aligned with the Standards. The first of five claims is "Claim #1: Students can read closely and critically to comprehend a range of increasingly complex literary and informational texts." The assessment targets define the task and the evidence required to meet the standard(s).

**GHR for Sample SBAC Assessment Target with Text:**
In late 2011, SBAC released annotated models that illustrate the proposed content of the assessments. A sample text for an eighth-grade assessment and the assessment target show how guided highlighted reading can help students analyze text to provide relevant and sufficient supporting evidence.

(See Reproducibles 9a-d for the student-prepared text of this passage with tasks and prompts for evidence.)

**Sample text: *The Meditations* by Marcus Aurelius**

1  A branch cut off from the adjacent branch must of necessity be cut off from the whole tree also.

2  So too a man when he is separated from another man has fallen off from the whole social
   community.

3  Now as to a branch, another cuts it off but a man by his own act separates himself from his

4  neighbor when he hates him and turns away from him, and he does not know that he has at the

5  same time cut himself off from the whole social system. Yet he has this privilege certainly from

6  Zeus who framed society, for it is in our power to grow again to that which is near to us, and

7  again to become a part which helps to make up the whole. However, if it often happens, this
   kind of separation,

8  it makes it difficult for that which detaches itself to be brought to unity and to be

9  restored to its former condition. Finally, the branch, which from the first grew together with the

10 tree, and has continued to have one life with it, is not like that which after being cut off is then

11 ingrafted, for this is something like what the gardeners mean when they say that it grows with

12 the rest of the tree, but that it has not the same mind with it.

**Assessment target:** In *The Meditations*, the author uses symbolism with the information about the branch and tree. Analyze the meaning of the symbolism and the author's purpose for using it. Use evidence from the passage to support your response.

**Guided highlighted reading for evidence:**

**Directions:** Using a copy of the numbered text and a highlighter, students will read the passage highlighting as the teacher prompts.

- In line #1, find and highlight the effect of cutting a branch from an adjacent branch. (Answer: ". . . cut off from the whole tree also.")

- In line #2, find and highlight the effect of a man separated from another man. (Answer: ". . . has fallen off from the whole social community.")

- In lines #4-5, find and highlight the result of the man's separating himself from his neighbor. (Answer: ". . . he has at the same time cut himself off from the whole social system.")

- In lines #6-7, find and highlight what is within man's power. (Answer: ". . . to grow again to that which is near to us, and again to become a part which helps to make up the whole.")

- In lines #8-9, find and highlight the effect of this separation if it happens often. (Answer: "... it makes it difficult for that which detaches itself to be brought to unity and to be restored to its former condition.")

- In lines #11-12, find and highlight the relationship of the grafted branch to the tree. (Answer: ". . . like what the gardeners mean when they say that it grows with the rest of the tree, but that it has not the same mind with it.")

- In line #12, find and underline what the author is symbolically implying about the separated man. (Answer: ". . . has not the same mind with it.")

**Sample analysis:**

This is an extended metaphor that compares a branch being cut from a tree to a man cutting himself off from society. The branch that is cut off symbolizes the man's act of cutting himself off from society. The author, Marcus Aurelius, states that by cutting himself off from his neighbor, the man is cutting himself off from society. Symbolically the man can rejoin society just as the branch can be grafted on to the original tree, but if the man separates himself from his neighbor often it will be difficult for him to return. By stating that the grafted branch (symbolizing the separated man) will not be of "...the same mind with it," Aurelius is implying that the man will not think like the rest of society because of his hatred for his neighbor. Aurelius is symbolically implying that this will negatively affect the unity of society.

**GHR for Sample SBAC Assessment Target with Two Texts**

**Sample text 1: "Meditation XVII" by John Donne**

1    No man is an island, entire of itself; every man is a piece of the continent, a part of the

2    main. If a clod be washed away by the sea, Europe is the less, as well as if a promontory

3    were, as well as if a manor of thy friend's or of thine own were: any man's death

4    diminishes me, because I am involved in mankind, and therefore never send to know for

5    whom the bells tolls; it tolls for thee.

**Sample text 2: *The Meditations* by Marcus Aurelius**

1    A branch cut off from the adjacent branch must of necessity be cut off from the whole tree also.

2    So too a man when he is separated from another man has fallen off from the whole social community.

3    Now as to a branch, another cuts it off, but a man by his own act separates himself from his

4    neighbor when he hates him and turns away from him, and he does not know that he has at the

5    same time cut himself off from the whole social system. Yet he has this privilege certainly from

6    Zeus who framed society, for it is in our power to grow

7    again to that which is near to us, and again to become a part which helps o make up the whole.
     However, if it often happens, this kind of separation,

8    it makes it difficult for that which detaches itself to be brought to unity and to be

9    restored to its former condition. Finally, the branch, which from the first grew together with the tree,

10   and has continued to have one life with it, is not like that which after being cut off is then

11   ingrafted, for this is something like what the gardeners mean when they say that it grows with

12   the rest of the tree, but that it has not the same mind with it.

**Assessment target:** The author of "Meditation XVII" and the author of *The Meditations* suggest that each individual is an important (*significant*) part of society. Show how this idea is developed in each of the passages. Use evidence from each passage.

**Guided highlighted reading for evidence:**

*Sample text 1:*

- In lines #1-2, find and highlight the relationship of man to the continent (Answer: ". . . a piece of the continent; a part of the main.")

- In line #2, in the metaphor the author is making, find and highlight the word that refers to man. (Answer: *clod*)

- In lines #2-3, find and highlight the words that show that the size of the piece doesn't matter. (Answer: *promontory*; *manor*)

- In line #4, find and highlight the effect on the author of the separation of a piece of land from Europe or the death of a man. (Answer: *diminishes me*)

*Sample text 2:*

- In lines #1-2, find and highlight the branch-to-man metaphor. (Answer: "A branch cut off from the adjacent branch must of necessity be cut off from the whole tree also. So too a man when he is separated from another man has fallen off from the whole social community.")

- In lines #3-4, find and highlight how the cutting of the branch is different from the separation of the man from his neighbor. (Answer: "Now as to a branch, another cuts it off, but a man by his own act separates himself from his neighbor. . . ")

- In lines #5-7, find and highlight the privilege given by Zeus to man. (Answer: "Yet he has this privilege certainly from Zeus who framed society, for it is in our power to grow again to that which is near to us, and again to become a part which helps to make up the whole.")

- In lines #8-9, find and highlight the effect of separating often. (Answer: ". . . it makes it difficult for that which detaches itself to be brought to unity and to be restored to its former condition.")

- In lines #11-12, find and highlight the implied comparison of the "ingrafted" branch's situation to the man's situation. (Answer: ". . . grows with the rest of the tree, but that it has not the same mind with it.")

**Sample analysis:**

The authors of these two meditations suggest that each individual is an important (significant) part of society by using extended metaphors. Donne compares man's significance to the significance of a piece of land, while Aurelius compares a man's significance in society to the significance of a branch to a tree. Donne implies that any man is a part of society by comparing a man to an island that does not stand alone but is part of a continent. Donne continues the metaphor by pointing out that if a piece of land of any size is washed away, the larger piece, Europe, is smaller, just as the death of a man diminishes society as a whole. Aurelius implies that man separating himself from society is like a branch being cut from a tree. The branch is cut from the tree while the man separates himself from society. When the branch is grafted to the tree "...it has not the same mind." The man who has separated himself from another man will not think the same even if he is reunited, and society will not be the same. Each man is a significant part of society; therefore, the loss of any man diminishes society and all other men.

# CHAPTER 3

## Using GHR to Assess Student Responses to Complex Text for Summary, Author's Craft, Vocabulary, and Multiple-Choice Questions

Guided highlighted reading is an appropriate tool to assess how well students can read and understand complex and difficult text, evaluate craft and structural decisions, comprehend and apply vocabulary, and respond to multiple-choice test questions. The following examples and suggestions for using GHR responses for both formal and informal assessments represent only a starting point.

As students acquire close reading skills for complex texts, the assessments will evolve—as will the opportunities for expanding on learning. For example, once students learn to summarize text, the teacher can build upon the skill by incorporating summary in other reading assignments.

*Guided Highlighted Reading* provides a sample passage at the end of this chapter along with several different types of tools that will help assess reading comprehension for the four purposes. (See Reproducibles 10a-f for a student-prepared sample passage, the prompts and rubrics for vocabulary, summary, writer's craft, and the multiple-choice questions & answers.)

Writing summaries and describing writer's craft lend themselves to evaluation with a rubric. The rubrics, which meet Common Core State Standards' expectations, can be used for formal and informal assessment. They give students the assignment's expectations, and they save time for the teacher. The data gathered can be applied to guide future instruction or used as a basis for a grade.

Both vocabulary and multiple-choice assessments afford opportunities for obtaining informal and formal assessment data to determine future instruction. To assess for depth of vocabulary knowledge and application, we suggest using the Cloze procedure (see Reproducibles 3b2, 6b2, 7b2, 10b2, and 12b2).

Finally, multiple-choice questions are simply assessed by evaluating student responses to practice test situations. Written to reflect the Common Core State Standards, the sample multiple-choice GHR questions enable teachers to determine whether a student has mastered that standard. In addition, practice with multiple-choice test formats familiarize students with—and prepare them for—the high-stakes, formal tests they will take throughout their school careers.

A management note: When at all possible, we encourage departments and/or grade level classes to set aside time for collaborative scoring of student work. Professional development time allocated to collaborative scoring will ensure consistency in your school/department.

## Adjusting the Level of Support

If students can already accomplish the purposes of GHR—that is, write an accurate summary, determine the author's craft choices, define vocabulary, and perform well on multiple-choice tests— the strategy is not needed for selections of that complexity and genre. It may be necessary, however, to use the strategy when the text complexity increases or a new genre is introduced.

The guided highlighted reading strategy provides as much support as students need. For example, some students may find it difficult to understand the text well enough to keep up with the class. If they have difficulty keeping up, slow down a bit at first, but do not slow down to the level of your slowest readers. GHR scaffolds for fluency.

If students have difficulty understanding how to highlight pertinent parts of the text, model the process by showing a correctly highlighted text passage on an ELMO or other projector. If this does not solve the problem, highlight the appropriate information as you read the prompt and project it for all students to see until students understand that skill.

When students can accomplish the purpose for which the GHR was given, it is time to begin to reduce the support that the prompts have given them.

The gradual release may begin by telling the students only the number of salient points in the first paragraph. After students have had a chance to find and highlight the text, read the prompts for that paragraph and let them check to see how many matches they have. Continue through the text with this type of support.

The next level of release would be to let the students know the number of prompted points in the complete text. After they highlight what they think are the important parts, read the prompts and have them check them against what they have selected. This could also be the basis for a good discussion if there are differences in what was selected.

Finally, when students have successfully responded to the GHR prompts for summary or author's craft, they are ready to create their own summaries or analyses.

Provide students with samples of possible responses. Discuss the effectiveness of the responses. If a rubric is used, apply it to a teacher model. Discuss what score it should receive, and have students defend the score they give.

They can practice by first talking with a partner about what they will write independently. Alternatively, they can write summary and craft responses in pairs. Share a few of the pair-generated responses with the class. Apply a rubric to the responses. Discuss what is missing and have students defend the scores they give.

When students score one another's work with the summary or craft rubric, they should defend the scores they give to their peers' responses. Class discussions of model summaries and written analysis of author's craft also help the students prepare their own work.

## Pre- and Post- Assessments

Pre- and post-assessment tests can document GHR results for each reading purpose. Students are given a complex text at their instructional level (i.e., text that is too difficult to read on their own without teacher support). They are asked to answer multiple-choice questions, define the identified vocabulary, write a summary, or analyze the author's craft. This becomes the pre-test data.

As the teacher, you are in the best position to decide when the students have reached a level of success with the applied GHR strategy. At that point, after the successful application of the strategy of GHR, students are given the assessment again. Data for this post-test is kept over time as the students progress through more and more complex text.

Of course, whether you are assessing for a grade or for instructional guidance, be sure to review the assessment criteria with the students. Students need to know your expectations.

**Cynthia:** I have found that parents appreciate the data I gather about their child's ability to read complex text. It often leads to discussion of complex text and parents' commitment to doing more reading at home. It is not unusual for parents to even ask for recommendations of books or ask for an extra class text that they can read and discuss with their child.

# Sample Assessment Passage with Rubrics

Sample summaries (p. 18 and p. 41) and descriptions of the author's craft (p. 21 and p. 44) have been provided. These samples, along with the rubrics, can provide a model for what is expected.

We illustrate the assessment component of GHR and conclude with a piece of text from ELA Appendix B of the Common Core State Standards. In the next few pages, the four types of assessment are applied to the same text, showing some of the possibilities for assessment using a single piece of text.

The assessments that involve writing and rubrics include sample responses so you can apply the rubric and attain a familiarity with the instrument for future scoring. The assessment component of GHR emphasizes the value of rereading the text, and the various lenses one can apply when reading a complex text closely and critically.

## Applying a Rubric for Summary

A rubric provides a framework for showing progress. The two rubrics provided in this chapter reflect the College and Career Readiness Anchor Standards for Reading noted in the Common Core State Standards for K-5 and 6-12.

Note that the language in the rubric for summary explicitly matches the language of the first and second standards.

> Please note the rubrics below are also in the Appendix as Reproducibles 11a-b.

**Common Core State Standards, College and Career Readiness Anchor Standards for Reading (K-5 and 6-12)**

> 1. Read closely to determine what the text says explicitly and make logical inferences from it; cite specific textual evidence when writing or speaking to support conclusions drawn from the text.
>
> 2. Determine central ideas or themes of a text and analyze their development; summarize the key supporting details and ideas.

# Rubric: GHR for Summary

### Correlated with the CCSS College and Career Readiness Anchor Standards
### for Reading (K-5 and 6-12)

| CCSS Anchor Standards for Reading | 3 Complete | 2 Partial | 1 Minimal | Score |
|---|---|---|---|---|
| 1. Read closely to determine what the text says explicitly and make logical inferences from it; cite specific textual evidence when writing or speaking to support conclusions drawn from the text. | **CCSS Anchor Standard for Reading 1**<br><br>Response:<br><br>• states what the text says explicitly.<br><br>• makes logical inferences and cites specific textual evidence to support conclusions drawn from the text. | **CCSS Anchor Standard for Reading 1**<br><br>Response:<br><br>• includes much of what the text says explicitly.<br><br>• makes some logical inferences and cites general textual evidence to support some of the conclusions drawn from the text. | **CCSS Anchor Standard for Reading 1**<br><br>Response:<br><br>• includes little of what the text says explicitly.<br><br>• makes few logical inferences and gives little support drawn from the text. | __/6 pts. |
| 2. Determine central ideas or themes of a text and analyze their development; summarize the key supporting details and ideas. | **CCSS Anchor Standard for Reading 2**<br><br>Response:<br><br>• summarizes using clearly identified central or main ideas.<br><br>• supports central ideas well with key details and ideas from the text. | **CCSS Anchor Standard for Reading 2**<br><br>Response:<br><br>• summarizes using partially or ineffectively identified central or main ideas.<br><br>• supports central ideas with some details and ideas from the text. | **CCSS Anchor Standard for Reading 2**<br><br>Response:<br><br>• summarizes using inaccurately identified central or main ideas.<br><br>• supports central ideas with few details and ideas from the text. | __/6 pts. |

Total: _____ /12pts.

This poem is a complex text suggested in ELA Appendix B for Grades 4 and 5:

"A Bird Came Down the Walk" by Emily Dickinson

**#1**
A bird came down the walk:
He did not know I saw;
He bit an angle-worm in halves
And ate the fellow, raw.

**#2**
And then he drank a dew
From a convenient grass,
And then hopped sidewise to the wall
To let a beetle pass.

**#3**
He glanced with rapid eyes
That hurried all abroad,
They looked like frightened beads, I thought;
He stirred his velvet head

**#4**
Like one in danger; cautious,
I offered him a crumb,
And he unrolled his feathers
And rowed him softer home

**#5**
Than oars divide the ocean,
Too silver for a seam,
Or butterflies, off banks of noon,
Leap, plashless, as they swim

**Sample Model Summary:**

A bird comes down a walk, eats a worm, and drinks the dew. (*explicitly what the texts says*) The bird is unaware of the human. (*inference*) However, once the bird senses the human, it appears nervous (*inference*), and the author offers it a crumb (*explicitly what the text says*). The bird opens its wings and flies away silently. (*inference*)

This text is a wonderful example to share with students as a scoring model because of the missing elements in the response. The teacher provides the summary model with a rubric and students carefully scan to detect intentional errors. This process opens the door for a discussion around evaluation. The atmosphere that student scoring creates is conducive for building a writing community. When you create your own models, you may occasionally fall short of meeting all the rubric's requirements to initiate a discussion.

**Sample Scoring:** The teacher's summary earns the first three points because it "states explicitly what the text says." It earns the second three points as the reader inferred the bird was uncomfortable with the author/human and supports the inference with "nervous" and "flies away" when offered a "crumb." So, the teacher earns a total of six points associated with reading anchor standard #1.

The teacher, however, intentionally left out the central or main idea and the supporting details needed to meet a six on the second anchor standard. The teacher would receive a two as the response "partially identifies a central or main idea" as the summary does infer the bird is wild and "supports" this idea "with some details from the text." So, in the second box the score would be a four. The total would be a ten out of twelve. A great discussion with students is how this could be teased out to be a twelve on the rubric.

**Cynthia:** If possible, teachers should consider meeting in grade levels or disciplines and participate in the common scoring of papers. This will enable a discussion of the rubric and the opportunity to modify and adjust it according to need. By applying the rubric to students' papers, teachers can create a common vision of complete, partial, and minimal responses.

## Applying a Rubric for Author's Craft

Provide students with copies of Reproducibles 5a-b ("Mining Informational/Narrative Text for Author's Craft"). These charts provide more support as students practice finding examples of author's craft in complex text.

Also note that the craft rubric directly aligns with five Common Core State Standards—the College and Career Readiness Anchor Standards for Reading (K-5 and 6-12) and the College and Career Readiness Anchor Standards for Language (K-5 and 6-12). They are the following:

CCR3. Analyze how and why individuals, events, and ideas develop and interact over the course of a text.

CCR4. Interpret words and phrases as they are used in a text, including determining technical, connotative, and figurative meanings, and analyze how specific word choices shape meaning or tone.

CCR5. Analyze the structure of texts, including how specific sentences, paragraphs, and larger portions of the text (e.g., a section, chapter, scene, or stanza) relate to each other and the whole.

CCR6. Assess how point of view or purpose shapes the content and style of a text.

CCL5. Demonstrate understanding of word relationships and nuances in word meanings.

# Rubric: GHR for Author's Craft

Correlated with the CCSS College and Career Readiness Anchor Standards for Language & Anchor Standards for Reading (K-5 and 6-12)

| CCSS Anchor Standards | 3 Complete | 2 Partial | 1 Minimal | Score |
|---|---|---|---|---|
| 3. Analyze how and why individuals, events, and ideas develop and interact over the course of a text. | **Anchor Standard for Reading 3**<br><br>Response expertly analyzes in detail where, when, why, and how events, ideas, and characters develop and interact. (Literature) | **Anchor Standard for Reading 3**<br><br>Response analyzes in some detail where, when, why, and how events, ideas, and characters develop and interact. (Literature) | **Anchor Standard for Reading 3**<br><br>Response analyzes with little detail where, when, why, and how events, ideas, and characters develop and interact. (Literature) | __/3 |
| 4. Interpret words and phrases as they are used in a text, including determining technical, connotative, and figurative meanings, and analyze how specific word choices shape meaning or tone. | **Anchor Standard for Reading 4**<br><br>Response:<br><br>• interprets words and phrases as they are used in a text (technical, connotative, and figurative).<br>• explains clearly how specific word choices shape meaning or tone. (Craft) | **Anchor Standard for Reading 4**<br><br>Response:<br><br>• interprets some words and phrases as they are used in a text (technical, connotative, and figurative).<br>• partially explains how specific word choices shape meaning or tone. (Craft) | **Anchor Standard for Reading 4**<br><br>Response:<br><br>• interprets few words and phrases (technical, connotative, and figurative).<br><br>• explains unclearly or incompletely how specific word choices shape meaning or tone. (Craft) | __/3 |
| 5. Analyze the structure of texts, including how specific sentences, paragraphs, and larger portions of the text (e.g., a section, chapter, scene, or stanza) relate to each other and the whole. | **Anchor Standard for Reading 5**<br><br>Response expertly analyzes the structure/organization of text (how specific sentences, paragraphs, etc., relate to each other and the whole). (Structure) | **Anchor Standard for Reading 5**<br><br>Response includes some analysis of the structure/ organization of the text. (Structure) | **Anchor Standard for Reading 5**<br><br>Response includes little analysis of the structure of the text. (Structure) | __/3 |
| 6. Assess how point of view or purpose shapes the content and style of a text. | **Anchor Standard for Reading 6**<br><br>Response expertly assesses how point of view or purpose shapes the content and style of a text. (Purpose) | **Anchor Standard for Reading 6**<br><br>Response does some assessment of how point of view or purpose shapes the content and style of a text. (Purpose) | **Anchor Standard for Reading 6**<br><br>Response does little assessment of how point of view or purpose shapes the content and style of a text. (Purpose) | __/3 |
| 5. Demonstrate understanding of word relationships and nuances in word meanings. | **Anchor Standard for Language 5**<br><br>Response demonstrates a clear understanding of word relationships and nuances in word meanings. (Word Relationships) | **Anchor Standard for Language 5**<br><br>Response demonstrates a somewhat clear understanding of word relationships and nuances in word meanings. (Word Relationships) | **Anchor Standard for Language 5**<br><br>Response demonstrates little understanding of word relationships and nuances in word meanings. (Word Relationships) | __/3 |

**Total:** _____ /15pts.

Below is a teacher's paragraph on the author's craft of Emily Dickinson's poem.

**Sample response by teacher on craft:**

The **genre** of the text is a poem that is divided into stanzas. The **organization** is chronological. The author **compares** the bird to a "fellow"; **metaphorically**, the bird is a gentleman and the bird's actions illustrate his manners. However, the author does observe the bird ate the worm "raw." In the third stanza, the author describes the bird's eyes using a simile ("like frightened beads") and a metaphor ("his velvet head"). In the fourth stanza, the poet attempts to interact with the bird by offering it a crumb. The bird flies away. The author **describes** this action of flight through **extended metaphor** ("And he unrolled his feathers/And rowed him softer home"). The final stanza uses **metaphors** to compare the flap of a bird's wings to an oar in water; both are smooth and "seam"-less.

Apply the craft rubric to the above response. The response receives a three for each of the four standards so it would receive a 12 out of 12 points.

## Assessing Vocabulary

To continue with Emily Dickinson's poem, "A Bird Came Down the Walk," as an example, you might note that your students find five challenging words in the poem: *convenient, abroad, stirred, banks,* and *plashless.* Once you've determined which words are challenging, you need to find synonyms or definitions for them and write a prompt for each word. For example:

In stanza #2, find and highlight the word that means "handy." (Answer: *convenient*)

Some quick ways to assess vocabulary are listed below:

- Ask students to write a two-sentence summary of the stanza or the poem using some or all of the challenging words that they have highlighted. Challenging words should be underlined. Note that this task can also be assigned to groups.

  Possible Answer: A bird was on "a *convenient* grass" where he ate a worm. The bird *stirred* when he sensed danger and flew in the air silently or *plashless* like a fish jumping silently.

- Students select two vocabulary words and create a six-word sentence, underlining the vocabulary words.

  Possible Answer: The butterfly *stirred* and flew *abroad*.

- Using the synonyms or definitions of the vocabulary words, students write a two-sentence summary of the passage and underline the synonyms and/or phrases that they used.

   > Possible Answer: A bird was on the *handy* grass near the sidewalk; it ate a worm. The bird made a *slight movement* when it felt danger and flew *without splatter or sound* into the air. (*convenient, stirred, plashless*)

Remember that students should be able to refer to the list of synonyms and definitions. Give them a copy of the list or write them on your whiteboard or overhead.

The above are merely suggestions; there are many other ways to assess vocabulary. For example, students can transform a prose or informational text sample into a cloze passage, completing the blanks with the synonyms. (See samples provided in Reproducible 10b1-2.) Teachers can also create multiple-choice questions regarding the vocabulary.

## Assessing Multiple-Choice Questions

Teachers can write the questions to reflect the ELA Anchor Standards or the reading standards of the grade level. For example, one such Standard is, "Read closely to determine what the text says explicitly and to *make logical inferences* from it; cite specific textual evidence when writing or speaking to support conclusions drawn from the text." So, a possible multiple-choice item for this standard might look like the following question:

In the poem, "A Bird Came Down the Walk," the poet compares the bird's eyes to

   A.    beads *
   B.    velvet
   C.    a beetle
   D.    a seam

If a significant number of students miss the same question, review the question's wording and the prompt(s) used to scaffold to the answer. Good discussions can easily emerge from such opportunities. Because fluency and speed often are an ultimate goal of this activity, it is important not to penalize students while they are scaffolding toward success. Instead, remove that scaffold over time, speeding up the reading gradually.

Many teachers find that students are best introduced to this activity by working in small groups. Also, encourage students to compete against themselves. Have students keep track of their improvement. For example, students could create a chart and note their scores, or they could even note the Standards that they missed. If a student has trouble with a particular standard then he may feel success as he notes his improvement with the standard.

## Final Note

This book was written in the hope that teachers will find this simple but effective guided highlighted reading strategy useful in their shared pursuit of literacy for all. Therefore, we leave you with one last stanza from Emily Dickinson:

### Hope

Hope is the thing with feathers

That perches in the soul,

And sings the tune—without the words,

And never stops at all.

# Appendix of Reproducibles

## GHR and the ACT's Six Elements of Complex Text

**Richness:** The text possesses a sizable amount of highly sophisticated information conveyed through data or literary devices.

**Guided Highlighted Reading for Summary and Craft**

**Relationships:** Interactions among ideas or characters in the text are subtle, involved, or deeply embedded.

**Guided Highlighted Reading for Summary and Craft**

**Style:** The author's tone and use of language is often intricate.

**Guided Highlighted Reading for Craft**

**Structure:** The text is organized in a way that is elaborate and sometimes unconventional.

**Guided Highlighted Reading for Craft**

## Complex Text

**Vocabulary:** The author's choice of words is demanding and highly context-dependent.

**Guided Highlighted Reading for Vocabulary**

**Purpose:** The author's intent in writing the text is implicit and sometimes ambiguous.

**Guided Highlighted Reading for Craft**

# The Six Elements of Complex Text Applied to an Excerpt from Patrick Henry's "Speech to the Second Virginia Convention" (1775)

## RSVP

**Relationships :** The relationships are deeply embedded. For example, the old image of America is one of weakness ("lying supinely on our backs") and the new image of America is "three millions of people, armed in the holy cause of liberty."

**Richness:** The richness of the text is sophisticated. The imagery abounds in the text and supports the relationship noted above. "Our chains are forged! Their clanking may be heard on the plains of Boston!"

**Structure:** The structure is unconventional. Five of the first six sentences of his speech are questions. This is not the typical start of a speech, yet it is quite effective rhetoric.

**Style:** Patrick Henry effectively varies his sentence length to manipulate the reader. His short sentences are powerful ("There is no retreat but in submission and slavery!"). He follows the sentences with longer sentences of elaboration. His word choice of "we" and "us" implies a "them" that is named only once: "British."

**Vocabulary:** The vocabulary of his speech employs context-dependent words (*irresolution, effectual*). These words are accessible to the reader through context, but require comprehension of text and root words.

**Purpose:** The purpose of the text is to persuade the delegates to form a militia in Virginia and to view England as the enemy—not the mother country. However, Patrick Henry never states his purpose; rather, he weaves it throughout the text as a call to arms.

RSVP is a mnemonic for the six elements of complex text: *Relationships, Richness, Structure, Style, Vocabulary, Purpose.*

## Excerpt

They tell us, sir, that we are weak; unable to cope with so formidable an adversary. But when shall we be stronger? (*Structure*) Will it be the next week, or the next year? (*Structure*) Will it be when we are totally disarmed, and when a British guard shall be stationed in every house? (*Structure*) Shall we gather strength by irresolution (*Vocabulary*) and inaction? (*Structure*) Shall we acquire the means of effectual (*Vocabulary*) resistance, by lying supinely on our backs, (*Relationships*) and hugging the delusive phantom of hope, until our enemies shall have bound us hand and foot? (*Structure*) Sir, we are not weak if we make a proper use of those means which the God of nature hath placed in our power. Three millions of people, armed in the holy cause of liberty, (*Relationships*) and in such a country as that which we possess, are invincible by any force which our enemy can send against us. Besides, sir, we shall not fight our battles alone. There is a just God who presides over the destinies of nations, and who will raise up friends to fight our battles for us. The battle, sir, is not to the strong alone; it is to the vigilant, the active, the brave. Besides, sir, we have no election. If we were base enough to desire it, it is now too late to retire from the contest. There is no retreat but in submission and slavery! (*Style*) Our chains are forged! Their clanking may be heard on the plains of Boston! (*Richness*) The war is inevitable and let it come! I repeat it, sir, let it come. (*Purpose*)

# Preparing Text for Four Different Purposes

1. Choose a complex text.

2. Prepare the text by numbering the paragraphs, stanzas, lines in the text, or breaks in a poem.

3. Determine which purpose(s) you want the students to practice: summary, author's craft, vocabulary, and/or answering multiple-choice questions.

4. Prepare the prompts based on the text and the purpose(s) chosen.

   a. **Summary**: Write a short summary to help you frame the prompts. Prepare prompts that will scaffold students to be able to:

      - restate in their own words what the text says explicitly

      - make logical inferences

      - cite specific textual evidence to support conclusions drawn from the text

      - determine central ideas

      - summarize the key supporting details and ideas

      *—From the CCR Anchor Standards for Reading #1 and #2 (K-5 and 6-12)*

   b. **Author's Craft**: First analyze the text for elements of craft including genre, organization, text features, point of view, mood, tone, figures of speech, and writing techniques like word choice. Use the information gained in your analysis to write a paragraph answering the question, "How does the author say it?" to help you frame the craft prompts. Prepare prompts that will scaffold students to be able to:

      - analyze how and why individuals, events, and ideas develop and interact over the course of a text

- interpret words and phrases as they are used in a text, including determining technical, connotative, and figurative meanings, and analyze how specific word choices shape meaning or tone

- analyze the structure of texts, including how specific sentences, paragraphs, and larger portions of the text (e.g., a section, chapter, scene, or stanza) relate to each other and the whole

- assess how point of view or purpose shapes the content and style of a text

*—From the CCR Anchor Standards for Reading #3, #4, #5, and #6 (K-5 and 6-12)*

c. **Vocabulary:** Handle this with Summary if there are only a few potentially troublesome words. The academic vocabulary is rarely defined in context and needs to be addressed before the student can do the close reading required. In this case, identify the words, find content-appropriate synonyms, and build prompts. Prepare prompts that will scaffold students to be able to:

- determine or clarify the meaning of unknown and multiple-meaning words and phrases by using context clues, analyzing meaningful word parts, and consulting general and specialized reference materials, as appropriate

- demonstrate understanding of word relationships and nuances in word meanings

- acquire and use accurately a range of general academic and domain-specific words and phrases sufficient for reading, writing, speaking, and listening at the college and career readiness level; demonstrate independence in gathering vocabulary knowledge when encountering an unknown term important to comprehension or expression

*—From the CCR Anchor Standards for Reading #4, #5, and #6 (K-5 and 6-12)*

    d.   **Multiple-Choice Questions:** Analyze the questions to determine how you can prompt students to find the answers in the text. Prepare prompts that will scaffold students to be able to identify and analyze the following:

- main ideas

- supporting details, examples, facts, claims, arguments, evidence

- organization and genre

- author's craft

- vocabulary important to the understanding of the text

- theme/central idea/purpose

5.   Give each student (or group of students) a copy of the text and a highlighter pen. In some schools, the same piece of paper is used to explore all four purposes; in that case, students can use different colored highlighters for each purpose, or they can combine underlining and circling text with highlighting for each successive purpose.

6.   Have students do a "fly-over" or skim to look for the topic and big ideas. Briefly give students the background information needed to understand the text and to help them access their prior knowledge.

7.   As you read a prompt, students re-read the text to respond to the prompts. At first, you will read the prompts fairly slowly; after multiple practices, you pick up the pace to build reading fluency and prepare students for time-limited multiple-choice assessments.

## *Common Sense* Text

1    The infant state of the Colonies, as it is called, so far from being against, is an argument in

2    favour of independence. We are sufficiently numerous, and were we more so we might be less

3    united. 'Tis a matter worthy of observation that the more a country is peopled, the smaller their

4    armies are. In military numbers, the ancients far exceeded the moderns; and the reason is evident,

5    for trade being the consequence of population, men became too much absorbed thereby to attend

6    to anything else. Commerce diminishes the spirit both of patriotism and military defence. And

7    history sufficiently informs us that the bravest achievements were always accomplished in the

8    non-age of a nation. With the increase of commerce England hath lost its spirit. The city of

9    London, notwithstanding its numbers, submits to continued insults with the patience of a coward.

10   The more men have to lose, the less willing are they to venture. The rich are in general slaves to

11   fear, and submit to courtly power with the trembling duplicity of a spaniel.

Reproducibles 3a-f feature an excerpt of Thomas Paine's *Common Sense* (1776).

## *Common Sense* **Reading Prompts for Vocabulary**

Directions: Read the following prompts while students highlight as directed.

- In line #1, find and highlight what the thirteen British settlements on the North Atlantic coast were called. (Answer: *colonies*)

- In line #2, find and highlight the word that means adequately. (Answer: *sufficiently*)

- In line #4, find and highlight the word that means obvious. (Answer: *evident*)

- In lines #5, find and highlight the word that means the result. (Answer: *consequence*)

- In line #5, find and highlight the word that means "wrapped up." (Answer: *absorbed*)

- In line #6, find and highlight the word that means loyalty. (Answer: *patriotism*)

- In line #10, find and highlight the word that means risk. (Answer: *venture*)

- In line #11, find and highlight the word that means deception. (Answer: *duplicity*)

## *Common Sense* Cloze to Assess Vocabulary Understanding

Directions: Write the appropriate word or phrase from the following list that is the correct synonym for each of the italicized words or phrases in the blank. To make sure that the synonym makes sense, read the sentence substituting the synonym for the italicized word or phrase.

venture                                        sufficiently

duplicity                                      absorbed

consequence                                    evident

colonies                                       patriotism

The infant state of the *British settlements* _____, as it is called, so far from being

against, is an argument in favour of independence. We are *adequately*_____

numerous, and were we more so we might be less united. 'Tis a matter worthy of observation that

the more a country is peopled, the smaller their armies are. In military numbers, the ancients

far exceeded the moderns; and the reason is *obvious*,_____ for trade being the

*result*_____ of population, men became too much *wrapped up*_____

thereby to attend to anything else. Commerce diminishes the spirit both of *loyalty* _____

and military defence. And history *adequately*_____ informs us that the bravest

achievements were always accomplished in the non-age of a nation. With the increase of commerce

England hath lost its spirit. The city of London, notwithstanding its numbers, submits to continued

insults with the patience of a coward. The more men have to lose, the less willing are they to

*risk*_____. The rich are in general slaves to fear, and submit to courtly power with the

trembling *deception* _____of a spaniel.

## *Common Sense* GHR Prompts for Summary

Directions: Read the following prompts as students highlight as directed.

- In line #2, find and highlight what the Colonies are ready for, according to the text. (Answer: *independence*)

- In lines #2-3, find and highlight what "we" would be if we were more numerous. (Answer: *less united*)

- In line #3, find and highlight what happens to armies when the number of people increases. (Answer: *smaller*)

- In line #5, find and highlight the consequence of population growth. (Answer: *trade*)

- In line #6, find and highlight another word for "trade." (Answer: *commerce*)

- In line #6, find and highlight what commerce diminishes. (Answer: " . . . the spirit both of patriotism and military defence.")

- In line #10, find and highlight what happens when men have more to lose. (Answer: " . . . the less willing they are to venture.")

- In lines #10-11, find and highlight what the rich are, in general. (Answer: " . . . slaves to fear.")

## *Common Sense* GHR Prompts for Craft

Directions: Read the following prompts as students highlight as directed.

- A metaphor is a figure of speech that compares two unlike things without the use of the words *like* or *as*. (example: Her hair was coal black.) In line #1, find and highlight the metaphor that the author uses to describe the colonies. (Answer: *infant*)

- In lines #2-3, find and highlight the sentence that means the same as, if there were more people in the colonies, the colonies would probably be more divided.
  (Answer: "We are sufficiently numerous, and were we more so we might be less united.")

- Personification is a figure of speech that gives human qualities to inanimate objects or ideas. In line #6, find and highlight an example of personification.
  (Answer: "Commerce diminishes the spirit both of patriotism and military defence.")

- Personification is a figure of speech that gives human qualities to inanimate objects or ideas. In line #7, find and highlight what the author is personifying.
  (Answer: " . . . history sufficiently informs us . . . ")

- In line #10, find and highlight a statement of cause and effect.
  (Answer: "The more men have to lose, the less willing are they to venture.")

- A metaphor is a figure of speech that compares two unlike things without the use of the words *like* or *as*. (example: Her hair was coal black.) In lines #10-11, find and highlight the first metaphor the author uses to describe the rich. (Answer: " . . . slaves to fear . . . ")

- A metaphor is a figure of speech that compares two unlike things without the use of the words *like* or *as*. (example: Her hair was coal black.) In line #11, find and highlight the final metaphor the author uses to describe the rich. (Answer: " . . . with the trembling duplicity of a spaniel.)

## *Common Sense* Multiple-Choice Questions

Directions: Choose the *best* answer for each of the questions. You may review the text you have highlighted.

1. According to this passage, what are the colonies ready for?

    A. consequences

    B. duplicity

    C. population

    D. independence

2. The word in this selection that means the same as trade is

    A. commerce

    B. spirit

    C. insults

    D. observation

3. How are rich people described in this selection?

    A. slaves to fear

    B. worthy of observation

    C. the bravest in history

    D. a consequence of population

4. Which sentence is a statement of cause and effect?

   A. "Men became too much absorbed"

   B. "We are sufficiently numerous"

   C. "In military numbers, the ancients far exceeded the moderns"

   D. "The more men have to lose, the less willing are they to venture"

5. In line #4, the word *evident* means

   A. risky

   B. obvious

   C. adequate

   D. unclear

6. In line #11, the word *duplicity* means

   A. loyalty

   B. double

   C. deception

   D. honesty

7. The figure of speech, "infant," in line #1 is an example of

   A. simile

   B. metaphor

   C. personification

   D. alliteration

## *Common Sense* Multiple-Choice Answers

Directions: Choose the *best* answer for each of the questions. You may review the text you have highlighted.

1. According to this passage, what are the colonies ready for?

   A. consequences

   B. duplicity

   C. population

   D. independence*

2. The word in this selection that means the same as trade is:

   A. commerce*

   B. spirit

   C. insults

   D. observation

3. How are rich people described in this selection?

   A. slaves to fear*

   B. worthy of observation

   C. the bravest in history

   D. a consequence of population

4. Which sentence is a statement of cause and effect?

   A. "Men became too much absorbed"

   B. "We are sufficiently numerous"

   C. "In military numbers, the ancients far exceeded the moderns"

   D. "The more men have to lose, the less willing are they to venture"*

5. In line #4, the word *evident* means

   A. risky

   B. obvious*

   C. adequate

   D. unclear

6. In line #11, the word *duplicity* means

   A. loyalty

   B. double

   C. deception*

   D. honesty

7. The figure of speech, "infant," in line #1 is an example of

   A. simile

   B. metaphor*

   C. personification

   D. alliteration

# "A Quilt of a Country" GHR Prompts for Vocabulary

Directions: Students are to go to the Daily Beast website to find Anna Quindlen's article, "A Quilt of a Country" (**www.thedailybeast.com/newsweek/2001/09/27/a-quilt-of-a-country.html**). Direct students to go to the last paragraph beginning with the word, "Tolerance" and copy and paste the paragraph into a word document, title the document, save the document, and number the six sentences.

Then using the highlighter pen on the computer, they are to highlight the words and phrases prompted by the teacher. Students can check their responses by sharing with other students, or the teacher can display his/her responses using a projector. In addition, the teacher could have students practice e-mailing their responses to the teacher.

Read the following prompts while students highlight as directed.

- In line #1, find and highlight the word that means "open-mindedness." (Answer: *tolerance*)

- In line #1, find and highlight the word that means "two or more groups living together." (Answer: *coexistence*)

- In line #2, find and highlight the word that means "not commented about." (Answer: *unremarked*)

- In line #3, find and highlight the word that means "extravagant." (Answer: *excessive*)

- In line #4, find and highlight the word that means "distrust." (Answer: *suspicion*)

- In line #5, find and highlight the word that means "loyalty." (Answer: *patriotism*)

- In line #10, find and highlight the word that means "crossbreed." (Answer: *mongrel*)

- In line #10, find and highlight the word that means "questionable." (Answer: *improbable*)

**About the Text**
Reproducibles 4a-e feature an excerpt from
Anna Quindlen's "A Quilt of a Country" (2001).

# "A Quilt of a Country" GHR Prompts for Summary

Directions: Students are to go to the Daily Beast website to find Anna Quindlen's article, "A Quilt of a Country" (**www.thedailybeast.com/newsweek/2001/09/27/a-quilt-of-a-country.html**). Direct students to go to the last paragraph beginning with the word, "Tolerance" and copy and paste the paragraph into a word document, title the document, save the document, and number the six sentences. Then using the highlighter pen on the computer, they are to highlight the words and phrases prompted by the teacher. Students can check their responses by sharing with other students, or the teacher can display his/her responses using a projector. In addition, the teacher could have students practice e-mailing their responses to the teacher.

Read the following prompts while students highlight as directed.

- In sentence #1, find and highlight the word that means "acceptance." (Answer: *tolerance*)

- In sentence #1, find and highlight what tolerance means.
  (Answer: " . . . letting others live unremarked and unmolested.")

- In sentence #2, find and highlight what "them" is referencing.
  (Answer: " . . . whoever is new, different, unknown, or currently under suspicion.")

- In sentence #3, find and highlight what patriotism is taking pride in.
  (Answer: " . . . this unlikely ability to throw all of us together in a country that across its length and breadth is as different as a dozen countries and still be able to call it by one name.")

- In sentence #4, find and highlight who is pictured on the "map of the world."
  (Answer: " . . . the faces of all those who died in the World Trade Center destruction . . . ")

- In sentence #5, find and highlight the kind of nation these people represent.
  (Answer: " . . . mongrel nation . . . ")

- In sentence #6, find and highlight when it is "a wonder."
  (Answer: " . . . when it actually works . . . ")

# "A Quilt of a Country" GHR Prompts for Craft

Directions: Students are to go to the Daily Beast website to find Anna Quindlen's article, "A Quilt of a Country" (**www.thedailybeast.com/newsweek/2001/09/27/a-quilt-of-a-country.html**). Direct students to go to the last paragraph beginning with the word, "Tolerance" and copy and paste the paragraph into a word document, title the document, save the document, and number the six sentences. Then using the highlighter pen on the computer, they are to highlight the words and phrases prompted by the teacher. Students can check their responses by sharing with other students, or the teacher can display his/her responses using a projector. In addition, the teacher could have students practice e-mailing their responses to the teacher.

Read the following prompts while students highlight as directed:

- In sentence #1, find and highlight the word choice the author uses for living together peacefully. (Answer: *coexistence*)

- In sentence #1, find and highlight the metaphor the author uses for the word tolerance. (Answer: " . . . a vanilla-pudding word . . . ")

- In sentence #3, find and highlight the partial definition of patriotism. (Answer: " . . . taking pride in this unlikely ability to throw all of us together . . . ")

- In sentence #3, find and highlight what America is compared to in the sentence. (Answer: " . . . a dozen countries . . . ")

- In sentence #4, find and highlight the imagery used to describe the physical traits of humans. (Answer: "skin color," "shape of the eyes and the noses," "the texture of the hair.")

- In sentence #4, find and highlight in the extended metaphor, what the photographs of the dead placed together would resemble. (Answer: " . . . a map of the world.")

- In sentence #5, find and highlight the author's word choice used to emphasize the mix of nations within one nation. (Answer: *mongrel*)

- In sentence #6, find and highlight the two descriptions of America. (Answer: "improbable idea," "wonder")

# "A Quilt of a Country" Multiple-Choice Questions

Directions: Students are to go to the Daily Beast website to find Anna Quindlen's article, "A Quilt of a Country" (**www.thedailybeast.com/newsweek/2001/09/27/a-quilt-of-a-country.html**). Direct students to go to the last paragraph beginning with the word, "Tolerance" and copy and paste the paragraph into a word document, title the document, save the document, and number the six sentences.

Choose the *best* answer for each of the questions. You may review the text you have highlighted.

1. Read the following phrase: " . . . standing for little more than the *allowance* of letting others live unremarked and unmolested."

   What does *allowance* mean in the phrase above?

   E. imposed handicap

   F. taking into account circumstances

   G. a regularly provided sum

   H. the act of permitting

2. Which of the following phrases is an example of a metaphor?

   A. " . . . the word used most often when this kind of coexistence succeeds"

   B. " . . . but tolerance is a vanilla-pudding word"

   C. " . . . letting others live unremarked and unmolested"

   D. " . . . when it actually works, it's a wonder"

3. Which of the following words does the author use to emphasize the mixture of nations?

   A. mongrel

   B. coexistence

   C. vanilla-pudding

   D. allowance

4. Which of the following words does the author use to emphasize the physical traits of humanity?

   A. imagery

   B. similes

   C. metaphors

   D. personification

5. What is the *primary* purpose of the selection?

   A. to persuade the reader that America is a wonder

   B. to instruct the reader in American history

   C. to entertain the reader with humor and word choice

   D. to inform the reader through analogies and story

# "A Quilt of a Country" Multiple-Choice Answers

Directions: Students are to go to the Daily Beast website to find Anna Quindlen's article, "A Quilt of a Country" (**www.thedailybeast.com/newsweek/2001/09/27/a-quilt-of-a-country.html**). Direct students to go to the last paragraph beginning with the word, "Tolerance" and copy and paste the paragraph into a word document, title the document, save the document, and number the six sentences.

Choose the *best* answer for each of the questions. You may review the text you have highlighted.

1. Read the following phrase: " . . . standing for little more than the *allowance* of letting others live unremarked and unmolested."

   What does *allowance* mean in the phrase above?

   A. imposed handicap

   B. taking into account circumstances

   C. a regularly provided sum

   D. the act of permitting*

2. Which of the following phrases is an example of a metaphor?

   A. " . . . the word used most often when this kind of coexistence succeeds"

   B. " . . . but tolerance is a vanilla-pudding word"*

   C. " . . . letting others live unremarked and unmolested"

   D. " . . . when it actually works, it's a wonder"

3. Which of the following words does the author use to emphasize the mixture of nations?

   A. mongrel*

   B. coexistence

   C. vanilla-pudding

   D. allowance

4. Which of the following words does the author use to emphasize the physical traits of humanity?

   A. imagery*

   B. similes

   C. metaphors

   D. personification

5. What is the *primary* purpose of the selection?

   A. to persuade the reader that America is a wonder*

   B. to instruct the reader in American history

   C. to entertain the reader with humor and word choice

   D. to inform the reader through analogies and story

# Mining Informational Text for Author's Craft ("How Does the Author Say it?")

## TEXT STRUCTURE

| Genre | Organization | Point of View | Tone/Mood | Text Features |
|---|---|---|---|---|
| • Online Article | • Thesis with Proof | • Date of Publication | • Persuasive | • Title (Question/ Statement) |
| • Essay | • Comparison/Contrast | • Source(s) | • Argumentative | • TOC/Index |
| • Article (Internet, Magazine Newspaper (News, Feature, Editorial/Op Ed) | • Cause/Effect | • Expert/Novice | • Propagandistic | • Illustrations/Pictures |
| | • Description/ Enumeration | • True/Misleading | • Matter-of-Fact/ Straightforward | • Heads/Subheads |
| • Scholarly Articles (Science) | • Chronological | • Reliable Narrator | • Humorous | • Margin Notes |
| • Pamphlet | • Problem/Solution | • Unreliable Narrator | • Disdainful | • Font Size |
| • Journal/Diary/Letter | | | • Informal/ Conversational | • Color |
| • Memoir/ Autobiography/ Biography | | | • Formal/Academic | • White Space |
| | | | • Scholarly | • Boldface |
| | | | • Pessimistic/Optimistic | • Italics |
| | | | • Biased | • Parenthesis |
| | | | | • Forward, Dedication |
| | | | | • Footnotes |
| | | | | • Charts |
| | | | | • Illustrations |
| | | | | • Diagrams |
| | | | | • Appendix |

## AUTHOR'S CRAFT

| Imagery/Figures of Speech | Writing Techniques |
|---|---|
| • Alliteration | • Catch Lead (Question) |
| • Allusion | • Examples Chosen for Audience Appeal/Interest |
| • Exaggeration/Hyperbole | • Explanation, Description, Definition, Step-By-Step How-To |
| • Irony/Sarcasm | • Show-Not-Tell |
| • Language: Precise, Scholarly, Scientific, Literary | • Precise/Detailed Examples in Proof |
| • Metaphor (Extended) | • Professional/Scientific Vocabulary/Domain-Specific/ Nomenclature (i.e., Latin And Greek), Foreign Words |
| • Onomatopoeia | • Punctuation For Effect (Ellipses, Parenthesis, Exclamation Points, Boldface, Italics) |
| • Over-/Understatement | • Technical Vocabulary |
| • Oxymoron | • Quoting Experts, Citing Books, Articles, Journals |
| • Personification | • Varying Sentence Length |
| • Repetition/Omission | • Word Choice |
| • Satire/Parody | • Use of Statistics |
| • Simile | |
| • Symbolism | |

# Mining Narrative Text for Author's Craft ("How Does the Author Say it?")

| Genre (specific) | Organization | Tone/Mood | Point of View | Notes |
|---|---|---|---|---|
| • Short Story | • Comparison/Contrast | • Satiric | • First Person | |
| • Novel | • Cause/Effect | • Humorous | • Third Person | |
| • Realistic Fiction (i.e., Adventure, Mystery) | • Description/ Enumeration | • Mournful | • Omniscient | |
| • Science Fiction | • Chronological | • Frivolous | • Limited Omniscient | |
| • Historical Fiction | • Story-Within-Story | • Mysterious | | |
| • Fantasy/Fairy Tales | • Time Shifts | • Dark | | |
| • Myth | -Foreshadowing | • Romantic | | |
| • Legends | -Flashback | • Pessimistic/ Optimistic | | |
| • Tall Tale | -Time Travel | • Childlike/Childish | | |
| • Epic | • Story Elements | • Biased | | |
| • Fable | -Characters | | | |
| • Parable/Proverb | -Setting | | | |
| • Pour Quoi Tale | -Conflict (Man v. Man, M v. Nature, Man v. Society, Man v. Self) | | | |
| • Journal/Diary | | | | |
| • Essay | -Rising/Falling Action | | | |
| • Allegory | -Climax | | | |
| • Drama | -Resolution | | | |

| Text Features | Imagery/Figures of Speech | Writing Techniques |
|---|---|---|
| • Title | • Simile | • Dialogue For Character/Plot Development (i.e., Soliloquy, Aside, Internal Dialogue) |
| • Chapters (TOC) | • Metaphor (Extended) | • Show-Not-Tell: Snapshots, Thought-Shots, Explode a Moment |
| • Illustrations | • Personification | • Strong Lead (Question, Humor) |
| • Font size | • Alliteration | • Varied Sentence Length |
| • Color | • Onomatopoeia | • Suspense Building |
| • White space | • Allusion | • Motif |
| • Boldface | • Satire/Parody | • Word Choice |
| • Italics | • Exaggeration/Hyperbole | • Minute Detail v. "Glowing Generalities" |
| Poetry | • Irony/Sarcasm/Oxymoron | • Punctuation for Effect (i.e., Ellipses, Parenthesis, Exclamation Points, Quotation Marks) |
| • Meter/Rhyme (Scheme) | • Repetition/Omission | |
| • Couplets | • Symbolism | |
| • Form (Sonnet, Epic, Ballad, Descriptive) | • Over-/Understatement | |
| Drama | • Vivid description | |
| • Acts, Scenes, Dialogue, Stage Directions | • Language (Precise, Poetic, Literary, Period) | |
| | • Cadence | |

## The Preamble of the *United States Constitution* Text

1    We, the People of the United States, in Order to form a more perfect Union, establish Justice,

2    insure domestic Tranquility, provide for the common defence, promote the general Welfare, and

3    secure the Blessings of Liberty to ourselves and our Posterity, do ordain and establish this

4    Constitution of the United States of America.

**About the Text**
Reproducibles 6a-f feature the Preamble of the
United States Constitution (1787).

## The Preamble of the *United States Constitution*
## GHR Prompts for Vocabulary

Directions: Read the following prompts as students highlight as directed.

- In line #1, find and highlight the word that means "to set up." (Answer: *establish*)

- In line #1, find and highlight the word that means "fairness." (Answer: *justice*)

- In line #2, find and highlight the word that means "home." (Answer: *domestic*)

- In line #2, find and highlight the word that means "shared." (Answer: *common*)

- In line #2, find and highlight the word that means "support." (Answer: *promote*)

- In line #3, find and highlight the word that means "obtain." (Answer: *secure*)

- In line #3, find and highlight the word that means "order." (Answer: *ordain*)

# The Preamble of the *United States Constitution* Cloze to Assess Vocabulary Understanding

Directions: Write the appropriate word or phrase from the following list that is the correct synonym for each of the italicized words or phrases in the blank. To make sure that the synonym makes sense, read the sentence substituting the synonym for the italicized word or phrase.

| | |
|---|---|
| promote | common |
| domestic | secure |
| ordain | establish |
| Justice | |

We, the People of the United States, in Order to form a more perfect Union, *set up*

_____ *fairness* _____, insure *home* _____ Tranquility,

provide for the *general* _____ defense, *support* _____ the general

Welfare, and *obtain* _____ the Blessings of Liberty to ourselves and our Posterity,

do *order* _____ and establish this Constitution of the United States of America.

## The Preamble of the *United States Constitution*
## GHR Prompts for Summary

Directions: Read the following prompts while students highlight as directed.

- In the title, find and highlight the country for which this constitution is being written. (Answer: *United States*)

- In line #1, find and highlight the first reason or cause for this document to be written. (Answer: " . . . to form a more perfect Union . . . ")

- In line #2, find and highlight the word that means "peace." (Answer: *Tranquility*)

- In line #3, find and highlight the word the authors use to indicate that this constitution is for future generations. (Answer: *Posterity*)

- In lines #1-4, find and *underline* the promises the authors/founding fathers imply will be realized when the Constitution becomes law. (Answer: " . . . to form a more perfect Union, establish Justice, insure domestic Tranquility, provide for the common defense, promote the general Welfare, and secure the Blessings of Liberty to ourselves and our Posterity . . .")

# The Preamble of the *United States Constitution* GHR Prompts for Craft

Directions: Read the following prompts while students highlight as directed.

- In the title, find and highlight the word that identifies the part or section of the document. (Answer: *Preamble*)

- In line #1, find and highlight the phrase (appositive) that identifies "We." (Answer: ". . . the People of the United States . . . ")

- In line #3, find and highlight what Liberty bestows or gives (personification). (Answer: *Blessings*)

- In line #4, find and highlight the formal words that the author chooses to use instead of ". . . to write or enact a law like a constitution." (Answer: " . . . ordain and establish . . .")

- Find and highlight the two words that are repeated for emphasis in the title, the first line, and the last line. (Answer: *United States*)

- Find and circle all the words the author capitalizes to emphasize their importance. These are words that would not usually be capitalized unless they were part of a title. (Answer: "Order," "Union," "Justice," "Tranquility," "Welfare," "Blessings of Liberty," "Posterity")

- Find and circle the punctuation marks the author uses to separate the promises. (Answer: four commas)

- Find and highlight the first period in the text. (Answer: After the last word–"America")

## The Preamble of the *United States Constitution*
## Multiple-Choice Questions

Directions: Choose the *best* answer for each of the questions. You may review the text you have highlighted.

1. The word "We" at the beginning refers to

   A. union

   B. people

   C. liberty

   D. posterity

2. The word "Justice" in the first line means

   A. support

   B. lawless

   C. secure

   D. fairness

3. The word "Tranquility" in the second line means

   A. promises

   B. peace

   C. general

   D. secure

4. The word "common" in the second line means

   A. ordinary

   B. truthful

   C. shared

   D. organized

5. The author indicates to readers that a word or idea is important by

   A. capitalizing it

   B. bolding it

   C. italicizing it

   D. underlining it

6. Which words does the author use to mean make a law?

   A. provide and promote

   B. form and insure

   C. ordain and establish

   D. secure and provide

7. How many sentences are there in this preamble?

   A. one

   B. two

   C. three

   D. four

## The Preamble of the *United States Constitution*
## Multiple-Choice Answers

Directions: Choose the *best* answer for each of the questions. You may review the text you have highlighted.

1. The word "We" at the beginning refers to

   A. union

   B. people*

   C. liberty

   D. posterity


2. The word "Justice" in the first line means

   A. support

   B. lawless

   C. secure

   D. fairness*


3. The word "Tranquility" in the second line means

   A. promises

   B. peace*

   C. general

   D. secure

4. The word "common" in the second line means

   A. ordinary

   B. truthful

   C. shared*

   D. organized

5. The author indicates to readers that a word or idea is important by

   A. capitalizing it*

   B. bolding it

   C. italicizing it

   D. underlining it

6. Which words does the author use to mean make a law?

   A. provide and promote

   B. form and insure

   C. ordain and establish*

   D. secure and provide

7. How many sentences are there in this preamble?

   A. one*

   B. two

   C. three

   D. four

## "Washington's Farewell Address" Text

1    Against the insidious wiles of foreign influence (I conjure you to believe me, fellow-citizens) the

2    jealousy of a free people ought to be constantly awake, since history and experience prove that

3    foreign influence is one of the most baneful foes of republican government. But that

4    jealousy to be useful must be impartial; else it becomes the instrument of the very influence to be

5    avoided, instead of a defense against it. Excessive partiality for one foreign nation and

6    excessive dislike of another cause those whom they actuate to see danger only on one side,

7    and serve to veil and even second the arts of influence on the other. Real patriots who may

8    resist the intrigues of the favorite are liable to become suspected and odious, while its tools

9    and dupes usurp the applause and confidence of the people, to surrender their interests.

**About the Text**
Reproducibles 7a-f feature an excerpt from
George Washington's "Farewell Address" (1796).

# "Washington's Farewell Address" GHR Prompts for Vocabulary

Directions: Read the following prompts while students highlight as directed.

- In line #1, find and highlight the phrase (two words) that means "deceptive tricks." (Answer: *insidious wiles*)

- In line #1, find and highlight the word that means "summon." (Answer: *conjure*)

- In line #2, find and highlight the word that we usually think of as meaning envy, but also means "watchfulness." (Answer: *jealousy*)

- In line #3, find and highlight the phrase that means "evil opponents." (Answer: *baneful foes*)

- In line #4, find and highlight the word that means "neutral," "independent," and "objective." (Answer: *impartial*)

- In line #5, find and highlight the word that means "favoritism." (Answer: *partiality*)

- In line #6, find and highlight the word that means "to move to action." (Answer: *actuate*)

- In line #8, find and highlight the word that means "conspiracies." (Answer: *intrigues*)

- In line #8, find and highlight the word that means "legally responsible." (Answer: *liable*)

- In line #8, find and highlight the word that means "hateful." (Answer: *odious*)

- In line #9, find and highlight the word that means "fools." (Answer: *dupes*)

- In line #9, find and highlight the word that means "to seize and hold." (Answer: *usurp*)

# "Washington's Farewell Address" Cloze to Assess Vocabulary Understanding

Directions: Write the appropriate word or phrase from the following list that is the correct synonym for each of the italicized words or phrases in the blank. To make sure that the synonym makes sense, read the sentence substituting the synonym for the italicized word or phrase.

| | | |
|---|---|---|
| conspiracies | responsible by law | move to action |
| hateful | fools | neutral |
| deceptive tricks | evil opponents | seize and hold |
| summon | favoritism | watchfulness |

Against the *insidious wiles* _____ of foreign influence
(I *conjure*_____ you to believe me, fellow-citizens) the *jealousy*
_____ of a free people ought to be constantly awake, since
history and experience prove that foreign influence is one of the most *baneful foes*
_____ of republican government. But that jealousy to be useful must be
*impartial* _____ ; else it becomes the instrument of the very influence
to be avoided, instead of a defense against it. Excessive *partiality* _____
for one foreign nation and excessive dislike of another cause those whom they *actuate*
_____ to see danger only on one side, and serve to veil and
even second the arts of influence on the other. Real patriots who may resist the *intrigues*
_____ of the favorite are *liable* _____
to become suspected and *odious* _____ , while its tools and
*dupes*_____ *usurp* _____ the applause and
confidence of the people, to surrender their interests.

# "Washington's Farewell Address" GHR Prompts for Summary

Read the following prompts while students highlight as directed.

- In line #2, find and highlight the warning Washington is giving to his audience. (Answer: ". . . the jealousy of a free people ought to be constantly awake . . .")

- In line #3, find and highlight what Washington identifies as " . . . one of the most baneful foes of republican government." (Answer: *foreign influence*)

- In line #4, find and highlight what Washington says jealousy must be to be useful. (Answer: *impartial*)

- In line #5-6, find and highlight the words that fit in the blanks in the following phrase: Excessive _____ for one foreign nation and excessive _____ of another. (Answer: "partiality," "dislike")

# "Washington's Farewell Address" GHR Prompts for Craft

Read the following prompts while students highlight as directed.

- In line #1, find and highlight how Washington refers to his audience. (Answer: ". . . fellow citizens . . .")

- In line #1, find and highlight the punctuation Washington uses to enclose a comment to his audience. (Answer: *parenthesis*)

- Washington's reference to jealousy is like personification when he says ". . . jealousy to be useful must be _____" (Answer: *impartial*)

- In lines #5-7, find and highlight the contrast that Washington makes. (Answer: "Excessive partiality for one foreign nation and excessive dislike of another cause those whom they actuate to see danger only on one side, and serve to veil and even second the arts of influence on the other.")

- In lines #7-9, find and highlight the sentence in which Washington warns Americans against getting too friendly with any other country. (Answer: "Real patriots who may resist the intrigues of the favorite are liable to become suspected and odious, while its tools and dupes usurp the applause and confidence of the people, to surrender their interests.")

# "Washington's Farewell Address" Multiple-Choice Questions

Directions: Choose the *best* answer for each of the questions. You may review the text you have highlighted.

1. The purpose or purposes of this speech is/are to

   A. say goodbye

   B. address foreign influence

   C. warn Americans to stay alert

   D. all of the above

2. Washington is warning Americans to

   A. influence others

   B. dislike other nations

   C. be constantly awake

   D. be partial to foreign nations

3. In this selection the word *jealousy* in the second line means

   A. watchfulness

   B. resentment

   C. impulsiveness

   D. impartiality

4. Washington is warning Americans against

   A. foreign influence

   B. causing danger

   C. disliking causes

   D. dangerous history

5. In this selection *impartial* means

   A. biased

   B. influential

   C. popular

   D. independent

6. The word in line #6 of this selection that means move to action is

   A. conjure

   B. actuate

   C. intrigue

   D. usurp

7. Washington refers to his audience as

   A. real patriots

   B. fellow-citizens

   C. free people

   D. all of the above

# "Washington's Farewell Address" Multiple-Choice Answers

Directions: Choose the *best* answer for each of the questions. You may review the text you have highlighted.

1. The purpose or purposes of this speech is/are to

   A. say goodbye

   B. address foreign influence

   C. warn Americans to stay alert

   D. all of the above*

2. Washington is warning Americans to

   A. influence others

   B. dislike other nations

   C. be constantly awake*

   D. be partial to foreign nations

3. In this selection the word *jealousy* in the second line means

   A. watchfulness*

   B. resentment

   C. impulsiveness

   D. impartiality

4. Washington is warning Americans against

   A. foreign influence*

   B. causing danger

   C. disliking causes

   D. dangerous history

5. In this selection *impartial* means

   A. biased

   B. influential

   C. popular

   D. independent*

6. The word in line #6 of this selection that means move to action is

   A. conjure

   B. actuate*

   C. intrigue

   D. usurp

7. Washington refers to his audience as

   A. real patriots

   B. fellow-citizens

   C. free people

   D. all of the above*

# "Mars: Extreme Planet" GHR Prompts for Summary

Directions: Go to the following site: **http://mars.jpl.nasa.gov/allaboutmars/extreme**. Make sure that you are on the "Summary" tab. Copy and paste the title and the first paragraph into a word document, name the document, save it, and number the five *sentences*. Then using the highlighter pen on the computer, highlight the words and phrases prompted by the teacher. You will be highlighting only in the title and the first paragraph.

- In the title, find and highlight the topic of the paragraph. (Answer: *Mars*)

- In the title, find and highlight the description of Mars. (Answer: *Extreme Planet*)

- In sentence #3, find and highlight the word the author uses to describe Mars as dry and lifeless. (Answer: *arid*)

- In sentence #3, find and highlight another name for Mars. (Answer: " . . . the Red Planet")

- In sentence #3, find and highlight the phrase the author uses to describe Mars as an unfriendly place. (Answer: " . . . offers few hospitalities.")

- In sentence #5, find and highlight the three things that a visitor would find on Mars. (Answer: " . . . the largest volcano in the solar system, the deepest canyon and crazy weather and temperature patterns.")

- In sentence #5, find and highlight the name the author gives to Mars. (Answer: " . . . the ultimate lonely planet . . .")

**About the Text**
Reproducibles 8a-d feature an excerpt from NASA's
Mars Exploration "Mars: Extreme Planet" webpage.

## "Mars: Extreme Planet" GHR Prompts for Craft

Go to the following site: **http://mars.jpl.nasa.gov/allaboutmars/extreme**. Make sure that you are on the "Summary" tab. Copy and paste the title and the first paragraph into a word document, name the document, save it, and number the five *sentences*. Then using the highlighter pen on the computer, highlight the words and phrases prompted by the teacher. You will be highlighting only in the title and the first paragraph.

- In sentence #1, find and highlight the word and punctuation the author uses as a warning. (Answer: "*Beware!*")

- In sentence #3, find and highlight the words the author uses to describe Mars. (Answer: "Arid, rocky, cold, and apparently lifeless . . . " and "the Red Planet . . .")

- In sentence #4, find and highlight a group the author refers to in order to make the writing more interesting. (Answer: "Fans of extreme sports . . . ")

- In sentence #5, find and highlight the three descriptive words the author uses to describe Mars' geography and weather. (Answer: *largest, deepest, crazy*)

- In sentence #5, find and highlight the vivid or strong verb the author uses to tell what Mars does. (Answer: *looms*)

# "Mars: Extreme Planet" Multiple-Choice Questions

Directions: Go to the following site: **http://mars.jpl.nasa.gov/allaboutmars/extreme**. Make sure that you are on the "Summary" tab. Reread the text. Choose the *best* answer for each of the questions.

1. What is the main idea of this paragraph?
   A. Mars has the biggest volcano
   B. Mars is an extreme planet
   C. Mars is rocky and cold
   D. Mars has the deepest canyon

2. What does the word "arid" mean in sentence #3?
   A. rocky
   B. crazy
   C. cold
   D. dry

3. Which word in sentence #1 is meant as a warning?
   A. future
   B. beware
   C. travelers
   D. rejoice

4. Which descriptive word or words does the author use to describe Mars' geography and weather?
   A. deepest
   B. crazy
   C. largest
   D. all of the above

5. In the last sentence, what vivid verb does the author use to tell what Mars does?
   A. looms
   B. goes home
   C. weathers
   D. is largest

# "Mars: Extreme Planet" Multiple-Choice Answers

Directions: Go to the following site: **http://mars.jpl.nasa.gov/allaboutmars/extreme**. Make sure that you are on the "Summary" tab. Reread the text. Choose the *best* answer for each of the questions.

1. What is the main idea of this paragraph?
   A. Mars has the biggest volcano
   B. Mars is an extreme planet*
   C. Mars is rocky and cold
   D. Mars has the deepest canyon

2. What does the word "arid" mean in sentence #3?
   A. rocky
   B. crazy
   C. cold
   D. dry*

3. Which word in sentence #1 is meant as a warning?
   A. Future
   B. Beware*
   C. Travelers
   D. Rejoice

4. Which descriptive word or words does the author use to describe Mars' geography and weather?
   A. deepest
   B. crazy
   C. largest
   D. All of the above*

5. In the last sentence, what vivid verb does the author use to tell what Mars does?
   A. looms*
   B. goes home
   C. weathers
   D. is largest

# GHR for Sample SBAC Assessment Target with Text

**Text:** *The Meditations* by Marcus Aurelius

1    A branch cut off from the adjacent branch must of necessity be cut off from the whole tree also.

2    So too a man when he is separated from another man has fallen off from the whole social community.

3    Now as to a branch, another cuts it off, but a man by his own act separates himself from his

4    neighbor when he hates him and turns away from him, and he does not know that he has at the

5    same time cut himself off from the whole social system. Yet he has this privilege certainly from

6    Zeus who framed society, for it is in our power to grow again to that which is near to us, and

7    again to become a part which helps to make up the whole. However, if it often happens, this kind of separation,

8    it makes it difficult for that which detaches itself to be brought to unity and to be

9    restored to its former condition. Finally, the branch, which from the first grew together with the

10    tree, and has continued to have one life with it, is not like that which after being cut off is then

11    ingrafted, for this is something like what the gardeners mean when they say that it grows with

12    the rest of the tree, but that it has not the same mind with it.

**Task:** In *The Meditations*, the author uses symbolism with the information about the branch and tree. Analyze the meaning of the symbolism and the author's purpose for using it. Use evidence from the passage to support your response.

## GHR for Evidence

Directions: Using a copy of the numbered text and a highlighter, students will read the passage highlighting as the teacher prompts.

- In line #1, find and highlight the effect of cutting a branch from an adjacent branch. (" . . . cut off from the whole tree also.")

- In line #2, find and highlight the effect of a man separated from another man. (" . . . has fallen off from the whole social community.")

- In lines #4-5, find and highlight the result of the man's separating himself from his neighbor. (" . . . he has at the same time cut himself off from the whole social system.")

- In lines #6-7, find and highlight what is within man's power. (" . . . to grow again to that which is near to us, and again to become a part which helps to make up the whole.")

- In lines #8-9, find and highlight the effect of this separation if it happens often. (" . . . it makes it difficult for that which detaches itself to be brought to unity and to be restored to its former condition.")

- In lines #11-12, find and highlight the relationship of the grafted branch to the tree. (" . . . like what the gardeners mean when they say that it grows with the rest of the tree, but that it has not the same mind with it.")

- In line #12, find and underline what the author is symbolically implying about the separated man. (" . . . has not the same mind with it.")

**Possible Answer:**

*This is an extended metaphor that compares a branch being cut from a tree to a man cutting himself off from society. The branch that is cut off symbolizes the man's act of cutting himself off from society. The author, Marcus Aurelius, states that by cutting himself off from his neighbor, the man is cutting himself off from society. Symbolically the man can rejoin society just as the branch can be grafted on to the original branch, but if the man separates himself from his neighbor often it will be difficult for him to return. By stating that the grafted branch (symbolizing the separated man) will not be of " . . . the same mind with it," Aurelius is implying that the man will not think like the rest of society because of his hatred for his neighbor. Aurelius is symbolically implying that this will negatively affect the unity of society.*

# GHR for Sample SBAC Assessment Target with Two Texts

## Sample text 1: "Meditation XVII" by John Donne

1    No man is an island, entire of itself; every man is a piece of the continent, a part of the

2    main. If a clod be washed away by the sea, Europe is the less, as well as if a promontory

3    were, as well as if a manor of thy friend's or of thine own were: any man's death

4    diminishes me, because I am involved in mankind, and therefore never send to know for

5    whom the bells tolls; it tolls for thee.

## Sample text 2: *The Meditations* by Marcus Aurelius

1    A branch cut off from the adjacent branch must of necessity be cut off from the whole tree

2    also. So too a man when he is separated from another man has fallen off from the whole

3    social community. Now as to a branch, another cuts it off, but a man by his own act separates

4    himself from his neighbor when he hates him and turns away from him, and he does not

5    know that he has at the same time cut himself off from the whole social system. Yet he has

6    this privilege certainly from Zeus who framed society, for it is in our power to grow

7    again to that which is near to us, and again to become a part which helps to make up the

8    whole. However, if it often happens, this kind of separation, it makes it difficult for that

9    which detaches itself to be brought to unity and to be restored to its former condition.

10   Finally, the branch, which from the first grew together with the tree, and has continued

11   to have one life with it, is not like that which after being cut off is then ingrafted, for this is

12   something like what the gardeners mean when they say that it grows with the rest of the

13   tree, but that it has not the same mind with it.

**Assessment target:** The author of "Meditation XVII" and the author of *The Meditations* suggest that each individual is an important (*significant*) part of society. Show how this idea is developed in each of the passages. Use evidence from each passage.

**Guided highlighted reading for evidence:**

*Sample text 1:*

- In line #1-2, find and highlight the relationship of man to the continent (Answer: ". . . a piece of the continent; a part of the main.")

- In line #2, in the metaphor the author is making, find and highlight the word that refers to man. (Answer: *clod*)

- In lines #2-3, find and highlight the words that show that the size of the piece doesn't matter. (Answer: *promontory*; *manor*)

- In line #4, find and highlight the effect on the author of the separation of a piece of land from Europe or the death of a man. (Answer: *diminishes me*)

*Sample text 2:*

- In lines #1-3, find and highlight the branch-to-man metaphor. (Answer: "A branch cut off from the adjacent branch must of necessity be cut off from the whole tree also. So too a man when he is separated from another man has fallen off from the whole social community.")

- In lines #3-4, find and highlight how the cutting of the branch is different from the separation of the man from his neighbor. (Answer: "Now as to a branch, another cuts it off, but a man by his own act separates himself from his neighbor. . . ")

- In lines # 5-8, find and highlight the privilege given by Zeus to man. (Answer: "Yet he has this privilege certainly from Zeus who framed society, for it is in our power to grow again to that which is near to us, and again to become a part which helps to make up the whole.")

- In lines #8-9, find and highlight the effect of separating often. (Answer: " . . . it makes it difficult for that which detaches itself to be brought to unity and to be restored to its former condition.")

- In lines #12-13, find and highlight the implied comparison of the "ingrafted" branch's situation to the man's situation. (Answer: " . . . grows with the tree, but that it has not the same mind with it.")

**Sample analysis:**

The authors of these two meditations suggest that each individual is an important (significant) part of society by using extended metaphors. Donne compares man's significance to the significance of a piece of land, while Aurelius compares a man's significance in society to the significance of a branch to a tree. Donne implies that any man is a part of society by comparing a man to an island that does not stand alone but is part of a continent. Donne continues the metaphor by pointing out that if a piece of land of any size is washed away, the larger piece, Europe, is smaller, just as the death of a man diminishes society as a whole. Aurelius implies that man separating himself from society is like a branch being cut from a tree. The branch is cut from the tree while the man separates himself from society. When the branch is grafted to the tree "...it has not the same mind." The man who has separated himself from another man will not think the same even if he is reunited, and society will not be the same. Each man is a significant part of society; therefore, the loss of any man diminishes society and all other men.

## "A Bird Came Down the Walk" Text

**#1**
A bird came down the walk:
He did not know I saw;
He bit an angle-worm in halves
And ate the fellow, raw.

**#2**
And then he drank a dew
From a convenient grass,
And then hopped sidewise to the wall
To let a beetle pass.

**#3**
He glanced with rapid eyes
That hurried all abroad,
They looked like frightened beads, I thought;
He stirred his velvet head

**#4**
Like one in danger; cautious,
I offered him a crumb,
And he unrolled his feathers
And rowed him softer home

**#5**
Than oars divide the ocean,
Too silver for a seam,
Or butterflies, off banks of noon,
Leap, plashless, as they swim

> **About the Text**
> Reproducibles 10a-f feature
> Emily Dickinson's "A Bird Came
> Down the Walk" (1893).

# "A Bird Came Down the Walk" GHR for Vocabulary

- In stanza #1, find and highlight the word that means worm used as fishing bait. (Answer: *angle-worm*)

- In stanza #2, find and highlight the word that means handy. (Answer: *convenient*)

- In stanza #3, find and highlight the word that means quickly looked. (Answer: *glanced*)

- In stanza #3, find and highlight the word that means moved. (Answer: *stirred*)

- In stanza #4, find and highlight the word that means careful. (Answer: *cautious*)

- In stanza #5, find and highlight the word that means ridge. (Answer: *seam*)

# "A Bird Came Down the Walk" Cloze to Assess Vocabulary Understanding

Directions: Write the appropriate word or phrase from the following list that is the correct synonym for each of the italicized words or phrases in the blank. To make sure that the synonym makes sense, read the sentence substituting the synonym for the italicized word or phrase.

| | |
|---|---|
| stirred | cautious |
| convenient | angle-worm |
| seam | glanced |

**"A Bird Came down the Walk" by Emily Dickinson**

**#1**
A bird came down the walk:
He did not know I saw;
He bit *a worm used for fishing bait* _____ in halves
And ate the fellow, raw.

**#2**
And then he drank a dew
From a *handy*_____ grass,
And then hopped sidewise to the wall
To let a beetle pass.

**#3**
He *looked quickly* _____ with rapid eyes
That hurried all abroad,
They looked like frightened beads, I thought;
He *moved* _____ his velvet head

**#4**
Like one in danger; *careful*_____,
I offered him a crumb,
And he unrolled his feathers
And rowed him softer home

**#5**
Than oars divide the ocean,
Too silver for *a ridge* _____,
Or butterflies, off banks of noon,
Leap, splashless, as they swim

## "A Bird Came Down the Walk" GHR Prompts for Summary

Directions: Read the following prompts while students highlight as directed.

- In stanza #1, find and highlight what came down the walk. (Answer: *a bird*)

- In stanza #1, highlight the line that implies the bird is unaware of the narrator. (Answer: "He did not know I saw . . . ")

- In stanza #1, find and highlight what was eaten raw. (Answer: *angle-worm*)

- In stanza #2, find and highlight the source of water. (Answer: *dew*)

- In stanza #2, find and highlight what was not eaten. (Answer: *beetle*)

- In stanza #3, find and highlight two visible signs the bird is uneasy. (Answer: " . . . rapid eyes . . . " " . . . stirred his velvet head.")

- In stanza #4, find and highlight what the narrator/poet offers the bird to eat. (Answer: *a crumb*)

- In stanza #4, find and highlight the phrases that indicate the bird flew away. (Answer: " . . . unrolled his feathers . . . " " . . . rowed him softer home.")

- In stanza #5, find and highlight the other flying creature of nature mentioned. (Answer: *butterflies*)

- In the last line of stanza #5, highlight the word that indicates birds and butterflies make no sound in flight. (Answer: *plashless*)

# "A Bird Came Down the Walk" GHR Prompts for Craft

Directions: Read the following prompts while students highlight as directed.

- When an author gives human characteristics to things that are not human, it is called personification. In stanza #1, find and highlight the word the author uses to personify the worm as a man. (Answer: *fellow*)

- In stanza #1, find and highlight the word that describes meat in the wild. (Answer: *raw*)

- When the beginnings of two or more words in a row sound alike, that is alliteration. In stanza #2, find and highlight the alliteration used in the first line.
  (Answer: " . . . drank a dew . . . ")

- In stanza #2, find and highlight the words that rhyme at the end of the lines.
  (Answer: "pass," "grass")

- In stanza #2, find and highlight the creature that the bird allows to pass. (Answer: *beetle*)

- When an author compares two unlike things using the words *like* or *as*, it is called a simile. ("Her hair is coal black" is a metaphor. "Her hair is as black as coal" is a simile.) In stanza #3, find and highlight the simile used to describe the bird's eyes.
  (Answer: " . . . like frightened beads . . . ")

- When an author compares two unlike things without using the words *like* or *as*, it is called a metaphor. ("Her hair is coal black" is a metaphor. "Her hair is as black as coal" is a simile.) In stanza #4, find and highlight the metaphor used to describe the bird opening his wings.
  (Answer: " . . . unrolled his feathers . . . ")

- When an author compares two unlike things without using the words *like* or *as*, it is called a metaphor. ("Her hair is coal black" is a metaphor. "Her hair is as black as coal" is a simile.) In stanza #4, find and highlight the metaphor used to describe the bird flying through the sky. (Answer: " . . . rowed him softer home . . . ")

- In stanza #5, line one, find and highlight the noun that stands for or symbolizes wings.
  (Answer: *oars*)

- In stanza #5, line two, find and highlight a word that means "the place where pieces are joined." (Answer: *seam*)

## "A Bird Came Down the Walk" Multiple-Choice Questions

Directions: Choose the *best* answer for each of the questions. You may review the text you have highlighted.

1.  In the poem, "A Bird Came Down the Walk," the poet compares the bird's eyes to
    A.  beads
    B.  velvet
    C.  a beetle
    D.  a seam

2.  In the line, "And then hopped sidewise to the wall/To let a beetle pass," what does the word pass mean?
    A.  to move by
    B.  to spread
    C.  to exchange
    D.  to take place

3.  What genre is this selection?
    A.  poetry
    B.  mystery
    C.  fable
    D.  myth

4.  Which of the following lines uses personification?
    A.  "He bit an angle-worm in halves/And ate the fellow, raw"
    B.  "And then hopped sidewise to the wall/To let a beetle pass"
    C.  "I offered him a crumb/And he unrolled his feathers"
    D.  "Than oars divide the ocean/Too silver for a seam"

5.  In stanza #5, which noun symbolizes wings?
    A.  oars
    B.  silver
    C.  seam
    D.  banks

# "A Bird Came Down the Walk" Multiple-Choice Answers

**Directions:** Choose the *best* answer for each of the questions. You may review the text you have highlighted.

1. In the poem, "A Bird Came Down the Walk," the poet compares the bird's eyes to:
   A. beads*
   B. velvet
   C. a beetle
   D. a seam

2. In the line, "And then hopped sidewise to the wall/To let a beetle pass," what does the word *pass* mean?
   A. to move by*
   B. to spread
   C. to exchange
   D. to take place

3. What genre is this selection?
   A. poetry*
   B. mystery
   C. fable
   D. myth

4. Which of the following lines uses personification?
   A. "He bit an angle-worm in halves/And ate the fellow, raw*"
   B. "And then hopped sidewise to the wall/To let a beetle pass"
   C. "I offered him a crumb/And he unrolled his feathers"
   D. "Than oars divide the ocean/Too silver for a seam"

5. In stanza #5, which noun symbolizes wings?
   A. oars*
   B. silver
   C. seam
   D. banks

# Rubric: GHR for Summary

### Correlated with the CCSS College and Career Readiness Anchor Standards for Reading (K-5 and 6-12)

| CCSS Anchor Standards for Reading | 3 Complete | 2 Partial | 1 Minimal | Score |
|---|---|---|---|---|
| 1. Read closely to determine what the text says explicitly and to make logical inferences from it; cite specific textual evidence when writing or speaking to support conclusions drawn from the text. | **CCSS Anchor Standard for Reading 1**<br><br>Response:<br><br>• states what the text says explicitly.<br><br>• makes logical inferences and cites specific textual evidence to support conclusions drawn from the text. | **CCSS Anchor Standard for Reading 1**<br><br>Response:<br><br>• includes much of what the text says explicitly.<br><br>• makes some logical inferences and cites general textual evidence to support some of the conclusions drawn from the text. | **CCSS Anchor Standard for Reading 1**<br><br>Response:<br><br>• includes little of what the text says explicitly.<br><br>• makes few logical inferences and gives little support drawn from the text. | ___/6 pts. |
| 2. Determine central ideas or themes of a text and analyze their development; summarize the key supporting details and ideas. | **CCSS Anchor Standard for Reading 2**<br><br>Response summarizes using:<br><br>• clearly identified central or main ideas.<br><br>• supports central ideas well with key details ideas from the text. | **CCSS Anchor Standard for Reading 2**<br><br>Response summarizes using:<br><br>• partially or ineffectively identified central or main ideas.<br><br>• supports central ideas with some details and ideas from the text. | **CCSS Anchor Standard for Reading 2**<br><br>Response summarizes using:<br><br>• inaccurately identified central or main ideas.<br><br>• supports central ideas with few details and ideas from the text. | ___/6 pts. |

Total: _____ /12pts.

# Rubric: GHR for Craft

Correlated with the CCSS College and Career Readiness Anchor Standards for Reading and the College and the Career Readiness Anchor Standards for Language (K-5 and 6-12)

| Anchor Standards | 3 Complete | 2 Partial | 1 Minimal | Score |
|---|---|---|---|---|
| 3. Analyze how and why individuals, events, and ideas develop and interact over the course of a text. | **CCSS Anchor Standard for Reading 3**<br><br>Response expertly analyzes in detail where, when, why, and how events, ideas, and characters develop and interact. (Literature) | **CCSS Anchor Standard for Reading 3**<br><br>Response analyzes in some detail where, when, why, and how events, ideas, and characters develop and interact. (Literature) | **CCSS Anchor Standard for Reading 3**<br><br>Response analyzes with little detail where, when, why, and how events, ideas, and characters develop and interact. (Literature) | __/3 pts. |
| 4. Interpret words and phrases as they are used in a text, including determining technical, connotative, and figurative meanings, and analyze how specific word choices shape meaning or tone. | **CCSS Anchor Standard for Reading 4**<br><br>Response expertly:<br><br>• interprets words and phrases as they are used in a text (technical, connotative, and figurative)<br><br>• explains clearly how specific word choices shape meaning or tone. (Craft) | **CCSS Anchor Standard for Reading 4**<br><br>Response:<br><br>• interprets some words and phrases as they are used in a text (technical, connotative, and figurative)<br><br>• partially explains how specific word choices shape meaning or tone. (Craft) | **CCSS Anchor Standard for Reading 4**<br><br>Response:<br><br>• interprets few words and phrases (technical, connotative, and figurative)<br><br>• explains unclearly or incompletely how specific word choices shape meaning or tone. (Craft) | __/3 pts. |
| 5. Analyze the structure of texts, including how specific sentences, paragraphs, and larger portions of the text (e.g., a section, chapter, scene, or stanza) relate to each other and the whole. | **CCSS Anchor Standard for Reading 5**<br><br>Response expertly analyzes the structure/organization of text (how specific sentences, paragraphs, etc. relate to each other and the whole.) (Structure) | **CCSS Anchor Standard for Reading 5**<br><br>Response includes some analysis of the structure/ organization of the text. (Structure) | **CCSS Anchor Standard for Reading 5**<br><br>Response includes little analysis of the structure of the text. (Structure) | __/3 pts. |
| 6. Assess how point of view or purpose shapes the content and style of a text. | **CCSS Anchor Standard for Reading 6**<br><br>Response expertly assesses how point of view or purpose shapes the content and style of a text. | **CCSS Anchor Standard for Reading 6**<br><br>Response does some assessment of how point of view or purpose shapes the content and style of a text. | **CCSS Anchor Standard for Reading 6**<br><br>Response does little assessment of how point of view or purpose shapes the content and style of a text. | __/3 pts. |
| 5. Demonstrate understanding of word relationships and nuances in word meanings. | **CCSS Anchor Standard for Language 5**<br><br>Response demonstrates a clear understanding of word relationships and nuances in word meanings. | **CCSS Anchor Standard for Language 5**<br><br>Response demonstrates a mainly clear understanding of word relationships and nuances in word meanings. | **CCSS Anchor Standard for Language 5**<br><br>Response demonstrates little understanding of word relationships and nuances in word meanings. | __/3 pts. |

**Total:** _____ /15pts.

## "Invasive Plant Inventory" Text

1     The Inventory categorizes plants as High, Moderate, or Limited, reflecting the level of each

2     species' negative ecological impact in California. Other factors, such as economic impact or

3     difficulty of management, are not included in this assessment. It is important to note that even

4     Limited species are invasive and should be of concern to land managers. Although the impact

5     of each plant varies regionally, its rating represents cumulative impacts statewide. Therefore, a

6     plant whose statewide impacts are categorized as Limited may have more severe impacts in a

7     particular region. Conversely, a plant categorized as having a High cumulative impact across

8     California may have very little impact in some regions.

**About the Text**
Reproducibles 12a-f feature an excerpt from
the California Invasive Plant Council's "Invasive
Plant Inventory" (2006-2010).

# "Invasive Plant Inventory" GHR Prompts for Vocabulary

Directions: Read the following prompts while students highlight as directed.

- In line #2, find and highlight another word for environmental. (Answer: *ecological*)

- In line #2, find and highlight the word that means result. (Answer: *impact*)

- In line #4, find and highlight the word that means taking over. (Answer: *invasive*)

- In line #5, find and highlight the word that means increasing. (Answer: *cumulative*)

- In line #7, find and highlight the word that means on the other hand. (Answer: *conversely*)

# "Invasive Plant Inventory" Cloze to Assess Vocabulary Understanding

Directions: Write the appropriate word or phrase from the following list that is the correct synonym for each of the italicized words or phrases in the blank. To make sure that the synonym makes sense, read the sentence substituting the synonym for the italicized word or phrase.

| | |
|---|---|
| invasive | impact |
| cumulative | ecological |
| conversely | |

The Inventory categorizes plants as High, Moderate, or Limited, reflecting the level of each species' negative *environmental* _____ impact in California. Other factors, such as economic *result*_____ or difficulty of management, are not included in this assessment. It is important to note that even Limited species are *taking over*_____ and should be of concern to land managers. Although the impact of each plant varies regionally, its rating represents *increasing*_____ impacts statewide. Therefore, a plant whose statewide impacts are categorized as Limited may have more severe impacts in a particular region. *On the other hand* _____, a plant categorized as having a High cumulative impact across California may have very little impact in some regions.

# "Invasive Plan Inventory" GHR Prompts for Summary

Directions: Read the following prompts while students highlight as directed.

- In line #1, find and highlight what the inventory is categorizing. (Answer: *plants*)

- In line #1, find and highlight the three inventory categories. (Answer: "High," "Moderate," "Limited")

- In lines #1-2, find and highlight what the categories reflect. (Answer: " . . . the level of each species' negative ecological impact in California.")

- In lines #2-3, find and highlight the factors that are NOT included in the inventory. (Answer: " . . . economic impact or difficulty of management . . . ")

- In line #5, find and highlight what determines whether a plant is categorized as High, Moderate, or Low. (Answer: " . . . cumulative impacts statewide.")

- In lines #5-8, find and highlight two examples in which the ratings may not reflect reality. (Answer: " . . . a plant whose statewide impacts are categorized as Limited may have more severe impacts in a particular region. Conversely, a plant categorized as having a High cumulative impact across California may have very little impact in some regions.")

## "Invasive Plan Inventory" GHR Prompts for Craft

Directions: Read the following prompts while students highlight as directed.

- In line #1, find and highlight the words the author capitalizes because they are names of plant categories. (Answer: "High," "Moderate," "Limited")

- In line #2, find and highlight the four words that identify the tone of this paragraph as academic and scientific. (Answer: " . . . species' negative ecological impact . . . ")

- In line #4, find and highlight the conjunction the author uses at the beginning of a sentence to signal contrast. (Answer: *Although*)

- In line #5, find and highlight the word the author uses to mean " . . . as a result . . . " The author uses this word to connect ideas between sentences. (Answer: *Therefore*)

- In line #7, find and highlight the word the author uses to mean " . . . on the contrary . . . " The author uses this word to signal contrast between ideas. (Answer: *Conversely*)

## "Invasive Plant Inventory" Multiple-Choice Questions

Directions: Choose the *best* answer for each of the questions. You may review the text you have highlighted.

1. The inventory is categorizing

   A. regions

   B. managers

   C. plants

   D. states

2. The categories of the inventory are

   A. limited

   B. high

   C. moderate

   D. all of the above

3. In this paragraph, the word *impact* means

   A. result

   B. solution

   C. score

   D. answer

4. In this paragraph, the word *invasive* means

   A. solving problems

   B. being warlike

   C. making better

   D. taking over

5. Which two different words does the author use at the beginning of sentences to indicate s/he is contrasting ideas?

   A. therefore, conversely

   B. although, conversely

   C. although, therefore

   D. other, although

6. Which word does the author use to mean *as a result* and to connect ideas between sentences?

   A. therefore

   B. although

   C. other

   D. conversely

# "Invasive Plant Inventory" Multiple-Choice Answers

Directions: Choose the *best* answer for each of the questions. You may review the text you have highlighted.

1. The inventory is categorizing

    A. regions

    B. managers

    C. plants*

    D. states

2. 2. The categories of the inventory are

    A. limited

    B. high

    C. moderate

    D. all of the above*

3. In this paragraph, the word *impact* means

    A. result*

    B. solution

    C. score

    D. answer

4. In this paragraph, the word *invasive* means

   A. solving problems

   B. being warlike

   C. making better

   D. taking over*

5. Which two different words does the author use at the beginning of sentences to indicate s/he is contrasting ideas?

   A. therefore, conversely

   B. although, conversely*

   C. although, therefore

   D. other, although

6. Which word does the author use to mean *as a result* and to connect ideas between sentences?

   A. therefore*

   B. although

   C. other

   D. conversely

## *Huckleberry Finn* Text

**#1** I had shut the door to. Then I turned around and there he was. I used to be scared of him all the time, he tanned me so much. I reckoned I was scared now, too; but in a minute I see I was mistaken — that is, after the first jolt, as you may say, when my breath sort of hitched, he being so unexpected; but right away after I see I warn't scared of him worth bothring about.

**#2** He was most fifty, and he looked it. His hair was long and tangled and greasy, and hung down, and you could see his eyes shining through like he was behind vines. It was all black, no gray; so was his long, mixed-up whiskers. There warn't no color in his face, where his face showed; it was white; not like another man's white, but a white to make a body sick, a white to make a body's flesh crawl — a tree-toad white, a fish-belly white. As for his clothes — just rags, that was all. He had one ankle resting on t'other knee; the boot on that foot was busted, and two of his toes stuck through, and he worked them now and then. His hat was laying on the floor — an old black slouch with the top caved in, like a lid.

**About the Text**
Reproducibles 13a-e feature an excerpt from Mark Twain's *Huckleberry Finn* (1885).

## *Huckleberry Finn* GHR Prompts for Summary

Directions: Read the following prompts while students highlight as directed.

- In paragraph #1, find and highlight why the speaker used to be scared of the man. (Answer: " . . . tanned me so much.")

- In paragraph #1, find and highlight why the speaker's "breath sort of hitched." (Answer: " . . . he being so unexpected . . . ")

- In paragraph #1, find and highlight what the speaker was thinking right after he saw the man. (Answer: " . . . I warn't scared of him worth bothring about.")

## *Huckleberry Finn* GHR Prompts for Craft

Directions: Read the following prompts while students highlight as directed.

- Dialect is defined as language that is different from standard English, for example using the word *ain't* instead of *am not*. In paragraph #1, find and highlight two examples of dialect. (Answer: "tanned," "reckoned," "see," instead of "saw," "warn't")

- In paragraph #2, line #1 find and highlight the words that Mark Twain uses to describe Huck's father's hair. (Answer: " . . . long and tangled and greasy . . . ")

- When an author compares two unlike things using the words *like* or *as*, it is called a simile. ("Her hair is coal black" is a metaphor. "Her hair is as black as coal" is a simile.) In paragraph #2, find and highlight the simile in the second line. (Answer: " . . . his eyes shining through like he was behind vines.")

- In paragraph #2, find and highlight the words the author uses to emphasize the whiteness of Huck's father's skin. (Answer: " . . . not like another man's white, but a white to make a body sick, a white to make a body's flesh crawl—a tree-toad white, a fish-belly white.")

- When an author compares two unlike things using the words *like* or *as*, it is called a simile. ("Her hair is coal black" is a metaphor. "Her hair is as black as coal" is a simile.) In paragraph #2, find and highlight the simile in the last line. (Answer: " . . . like a lid.")

## *Huckleberry Finn* ACT Sample Questions

Directions: Read the passage again and choose the best answer to each question. You may refer to the passage as often as necessary to answer the questions.

1. The speaker's state of mind in the first paragraph is best described as

   A. terrified

   B. surprised, but not scared

   C. terrified at first, but then delighted

   D. unaltered

2. The second paragraph differs from the first paragraph because several times it uses

   A. personification

   B. denotative language

   C. dialogue

   D. simile and metaphor

3. The description in the second paragraph makes the unknown man appear

   A. pathetic

   B. intriguing

   C. repulsive

   D. annoying

# *Huckleberry Finn* ACT Sample Answers

Directions: Read the passage again and choose the best answer to each question. You may refer to the passage as often as necessary to answer the questions.

1. The speaker's state of mind in the first paragraph is best described as

    A. terrified

    B. surprised, but not scared*

    C. terrified at first, but then delighted

    D. unaltered

2. The second paragraph differs from the first paragraph because several times it uses

    A. personification

    B. denotative language

    C. dialogue

    D. simile and metaphor*

3. The description in the second paragraph makes the unknown man appear

    A. pathetic

    B. intriguing

    C. repulsive*

    D. annoying

## Narrative of the Life of Frederick Douglass, an American Slave Text

1   In the same book, I met with one of Sheridan's mighty speeches on and in behalf of Catholic

2   emancipation. These were choice documents to me. I read them over and over again with

3   unabated interest. They gave tongue to interesting thoughts of my own soul, which had

4   frequently flashed through my mind, and died away for want of utterance. The moral which I

5   gained from the dialogue was the power of truth over the conscience of even a slaveholder.

6   What I got from Sheridan was a bold denunciation of slavery, and a powerful vindication of

7   human rights. The reading of these documents enabled me to utter my thoughts, and to meet the

8   arguments brought forward to sustain slavery; but while they relieved me of one difficulty, they

9   bought on another even more painful than the one of which I was relieved. The more I read, the

10  more I was led to abhor and detest my enslavers. I could regard them in no other light than a

11  band of successful robbers, who had left their homes, and gone to Africa, and stolen us from

12  our homes, and in a strange land deduced us to slavery. I loathed them as being the meanest as

13  well as the most wicked of men. As I read and contemplated the subject, behold! That very

14  discontentment which Master Hugh had predicted would follow my learning to read had

15  already come, to torment and sting my soul to unutterable anguish. As I writhed under it, I

16  would at times feel that learning to read had been a curse rather than a blessing. It had given

17  me a view of my wretched condition, without the remedy. It opened my eyes to the horrible

18  pit, but to no ladder upon which to get out. In moments of agony, I envied my fellow-slaves

19  for their stupidity. I have often wished myself a beast. I preferred the condition of the meanest

20  reptile to my own. Anything, no matter what, to get rid of thinking! It was this everlasting

21  thinking of my condition that tormented me. There was no getting rid of it. It was pressed

22  upon me by every object within sight or hearing, animate or inanimate. The silver trump to

23  freedom had roused my soul to eternal wakefulness. Freedom now appeared, to disappear no

24  more forever. It was heard in every sound and seen in everything. It was ever present to

25  torment me with a sense of my wretched condition. I saw nothing without seeing it, I heard

26  nothing without hearing it, and felt nothing without feeling it. It looked from every star, it smiled

27  in every calm, breathed in every wind, and moved in every storm.

### About the Text
Reproducibles 14a-f feature an excerpt from Frederick Douglass' *Narrative of the Life of Frederick Douglass an American Slave, Written by Himself* (1845).

## *Narrative of the Life of Frederick Douglass, an American Slave*
## GHR Prompts for Vocabulary

Directions: Read the following prompts while students highlight as directed.

- In line #2, find and highlight the word that means "freedom." (Answer: *emancipation*)

- In line #3, find and highlight the word that means "unceasing." (Answer: *unabated*)

- In line #4, find and highlight the word that means "communication." (Answer: *utterance*)

- In line #5, find and highlight the word that means "morals." (Answer: *conscience*)

- In line #6, find and highlight the word that means "accusation." (Answer: *denunciation*)

- In line #6, find and highlight the word that means "justification." (Answer: *vindication*)

- In line #15, find and highlight the word that means "struggled." (Answer: *writhed*)

## *Narrative of the Life of Frederick Douglass, an American Slave* GHR Prompts for Summary

Directions: Read the following prompts while students answer.

- In line #1, find and highlight what specific text Frederick Douglass read over and over. (Answer " . . . one of Sheridan's mighty speeches . . . ")

- In line #3, find and highlight what the words gave tongue to for Frederick Douglass. (Answer: " . . . thoughts of my own soul . . . ")

- In line #5, find and highlight the moral Frederick Douglass gained from his reading. (Answer: " . . . power of truth over the conscience . . . ")

- In lines #6-7, find and highlight the two beliefs that Frederick Douglass gained from his readings of Sheridan. (Answer: " . . . bold denunciation of slavery, and a powerful vindication of human rights.")

- In line #7, find and highlight what the reading enabled Frederick Douglass to do. (Answer: " . . . utter my thoughts and to meet the arguments . . . ")

- In line #10, find and highlight what emotions the reading evoked in Frederick Douglass. (Answer: " . . . to abhor and detest my enslavers.")

- In line #14, find and highlight what Frederick Douglass sometimes thought of as a curse. (Answer: " . . . learning to read . . . ")

- In line #20, find and highlight why Frederick Douglass often wished himself stupid or a beast. (Answer: " . . . to get rid of thinking!")

- In line #23, find and highlight the idea that haunted Frederick Douglass at all times. (Answer: *freedom*)

## *Narrative of the Life of Frederick Douglass, an American Slave* GHR Prompts for Craft

Directions: Read the following prompts while students highlight as directed.

- In line #3, find and highlight the word the author uses to represent voice. (Answer: *tongue*)

- In lines #6-7, find and highlight the phrases that summarize the two components of Sheridan's argument: (Answer: " . . . a bold denunciation of slavery . . . " " . . . a powerful vindication of human rights.")

- In lines #7-10, find and highlight two effects that resulted from Frederick Douglass' reading. (Answer: " . . . to utter my thoughts, and to meet the arguments brought forward to sustain slavery . . . " " . . . to abhor and detest my enslavers.")

- A metaphor is a figure of speech that compares two unlike things without the use of the words *like* or *as*. (example: Her hair was coal black.) In line #11, find and highlight Douglass' metaphor for his enslavers. (Answer: " . . . successful robbers . . . ")

- In line #11, find and highlight an allusion to an historical event that continued for many years. (Answer: " . . . gone to Africa, and stolen us . . . ")

- In line #16, find and highlight the two words that are opposite in meaning that the author places near each other to emphasize the contrast: (Answer: "curse", "blessing")

- Trumpets are often associated with awakening. In line #22, find and highlight an archaic word that means trumpet. (Answer: *trump*)

- In lines #23-27, find and highlight the word *freedom*, which is being personified. Then find and highlight the six times the word "it" is used to refer to freedom.

## Narrative of the Life of Frederick Douglass, an American Slave
## Multiple-Choice Questions

Directions: Choose the *best* answer for each of the questions. You may review the text you have highlighted.

1. Read the following:

"They *gave tongue* to interesting thoughts of my own soul, which had frequently flashed through my mind, and died away for want of utterance."

What does *gave tongue* mean in the sentence?

   A. offered food

   B. provided words

   C. supplied thinking

   D. granted reflection

2. Considering what he wrote about in this selection, Frederick Douglass would *most likely* agree with which of the following statements?

   A. It is more painful to be conscious of injustice than it is to be ignorant of it

   B. It is necessary to spread the word of freedom to others if change is to occur

   C. It is possible to change the world through the words of certain texts

   D. It is more just to offer freedom to all than it is to just offer freedom to the literate

3. Considering the title of this selection, what genre does this selection represent?

   A. autobiography

   B. historical fiction

   C. biography

   D. science fiction

4. What is the meaning of *denunciation* in line #6?

   A. accusation

   B. conscience

   C. emancipation

   D. vindication

5. What organizational structure does the author use in lines #7- 10?

   A. compare and contrast

   B. cause and effect

   C. chronological

   D. problem and solution

6. The author concludes the selection (lines #23-27) with the literary device of

   A. personification

   B. analogy

   C. metaphor

   D. simile

## Narrative of the Life of Frederick Douglass, an American Slave
## Multiple-Choice Answers

Directions: Choose the *best* answer for each of the questions. You may review the text you have highlighted.

1. Read the following:

"They *gave tongue* to interesting thoughts of my own soul, which had frequently flashed through my mind, and died away for want of utterance."

What does *gave tongue* mean in the sentence?

    A. offered food

    B. provided words*

    C. supplied thinking

    D. granted reflection


2. Considering what he wrote about in this selection, Frederick Douglass would *most likely* agree with which of the following statements?

    A. It is more painful to be conscious of injustice than it is to be ignorant of it*

    B. It is necessary to spread the word of freedom to others if change is to occur

    C. It is possible to change the world through the words of certain texts

    D. It is more just to offer freedom to all than it is to just offer freedom to the literate

3.  Considering the title of this selection, what genre does this selection represent?

    A.  autobiography*

    B.  historical fiction

    C.  biography

    D.  science fiction

4.  What is the meaning of *denunciation* in line #6?

    A.  accusation*

    B.  conscience

    C.  emancipation

    D.  vindication

5.  What organizational structure does the author use in lines #7-10?

    A.  compare and contrast

    B.  cause and effect*

    C.  chronological

    D.  problem and solution

6.  The author concludes the selection (lines #23-27) with the literary device of

    A.  personification*

    B.  analogy

    C.  metaphor

    D.  simile

# "Speech to the Second Virginia Convention" Text

1    They tell us, sir, that we are weak; unable to cope with so formidable an adversary. But when

2    shall we be stronger? Will it be the next week, or the next year? Will it be when we are totally

3    disarmed, and when a British guard shall be stationed in every house? Shall we gather strength

4    by irresolution and inaction? Shall we acquire the means of effectual resistance, by lying

5    supinely on our backs, and hugging the delusive phantom of hope, until our enemies shall have

6    bound us hand and foot? Sir, we are not weak if we make a proper use of those means which the

7    God of nature hath placed in our power. Three millions of people, armed in the holy cause of

8    liberty, and in such a country as that which we possess, are invincible by any force which our

9    enemy can send against us. Besides, sir, we shall not fight our battles alone. There is a just God

10    who presides over the destinies of nations; and who will raise up friends to fight our battles for

11    us. The battle, sir, is not to the strong alone; it is to the vigilant, the active, the brave. Besides, sir,

12    we have no election. If we were base enough to desire it, it is now too late to retire from the

13    contest. There is no retreat but in submission and slavery! Our chains are forged! Their clanking

14    may be heard on the plains of Boston! The war is inevitable and let it come! I repeat it, sir, let

15    it come.

**About the Text**
Reproducibles 15a-f feature an excerpt from Patrick Henry's "Speech to the Second Virginia Convention" (1775).

## "Speech to the Second Virginia Convention" GHR Prompts for Vocabulary

Directions: Read the following prompts while students highlight as directed.

- In line #1, find and highlight the word that means causing fear or dread. (Answer: *formidable*)

- In line #1, find and highlight the word that means opponent or enemy. (Answer: *adversary*)

- In line #4, find and highlight the word that means indecision. (Answer: *irresolution*)

- In line #4, find and highlight the word that means capable. (Answer: *effectual*)

- In line #5, find and highlight the word that means lying on the back or having the face upward. (Answer: *supinely*)

- In line #5, find and highlight the word that means misleading. (Answer: *delusive*)

- In line #8, find and highlight the word that means unbeatable (Answer: *invincible*)

- In line #11, find and highlight the word that means watchful (Answer: *vigilant*)

- In line #13, find and highlight the word that means formed by a process like heating and shaping. (Answer: *forged*)

## "Speech to the Second Virginia Convention" GHR Prompts for Summary

Directions: Read the following prompts while students highlight as directed.

- In line #1, find and highlight the first claim that is being made.
  (Answer: " . . . we are weak . . . ")

- In lines #1-2, find and highlight the first question.
  (Answer: "But when shall we be stronger?")

- In line #3, find and highlight what could happen.
  (Answer: " . . . a British guard shall be stationed in every house . . . ")

- In lines #5-6, find and highlight what else could happen if they lie on their backs.
  (Answer: " . . . our enemies shall have bound us hand and foot . . . ")

- In line #6, find and highlight how Patrick Henry answers the claim that they are weak.
  (Answer: " . . . we are not weak . . . ")

- In line #10, find and highlight who will help the colonists fight their battles.
  (Answer: *friends*)

- In line #14, find and highlight what is coming for sure. (Answer: *war*)

# "Speech to the Second Virginia Convention" GHR Prompts for Craft

Directions: Read the following prompts while students highlight as directed.

- In lines #1-14, find and highlight the word that is repeated five times. (Answer: *sir*)

- In line #1, find and highlight the words the author uses to describe the enemy. (Answer: " . . . so formidable an adversary.")

- In lines #1-2, find and highlight the first rhetorical question—a question to which the speaker does not expect an answer. (Answer: "But when shall we be stronger?")

- In lines #4-6, find and highlight the imagery the speaker uses to emphasize that the colonists need to stand up instead of lying down for their rights. (Answer: " . . . by lying supinely on our backs, and hugging the delusive phantom of hope, until our enemies shall have bound us hand and foot . . . ")

- In line #6, find and highlight the answer to the original claim of weakness. (Answer: " . . . we are not weak . . . ")

- In line #11, find and highlight who the author suggests will be the winner of the battle. (Answer: "The battle, sir, is not to the strong alone; it is to the vigilant, the active, the brave.")

- In lines #13-14, find and highlight the extended metaphor. (Answer: "Our chains are forged! Their clanking may be heard on the plains of Boston!")

- In lines #14-15, find and highlight the speaker's call to action. (Answer: "The war is inevitable and let it come! I repeat it, sir, let it come.")

# "Speech to the Second Virginia Convention"
# Multiple-Choice Questions

Directions: Choose the *best* answer for each of the questions. You may review the text you have highlighted.

1. The main purpose of this speech is to:

   A. Stop people from lying down

   B. Show the inevitability of war

   C. Encourage Americans to fight their battles alone

   D. Prove that three million Americans are weak

2. According to this passage, who will help the Americans fight their battles?

   A. the British

   B. friends

   C. a formidable adversary

   D. King George

3. In line #8 the word *invincible* means

   A. unbeatable

   B. convincing

   C. friendly

   D. destructive

4. The author suggests that the winner of the battle will be

    A. the vigilant

    B. the active

    C. the brave

    D. all of the above

5. The word in the selection that means opponent or enemy is

    A. adversary

    B. supinely

    C. vigilant

    D. forged

6. Which word in line #11 means watchful and careful?

    A. brave

    B. active

    C. vigilant

    D. strong

7. Patrick Henry's call to action is

    A. "Shall we gather strength by irresolution and inaction?"

    B. "... sir, we shall not fight our battles alone."

    C. "The war is inevitable and let it come!"

    D. "They tell us, sir, that we are weak ..."

# "Speech to the Second Virginia Convention" Multiple-Choice Answers

Directions: Choose the *best* answer for each of the questions. You may review the text you have highlighted.

1. The main purpose of this speech is to:

   A. Stop people from lying down

   B. Show the inevitability of war*

   C. Encourage Americans to fight their battles alone

   D. Prove that three million Americans are weak

2. According to this passage, who will help the Americans fight their battles?

   A. the British

   B. friends*

   C. a formidable adversary

   D. King George

3. In line #8 the word *invincible* means

   A. unbeatable*

   B. convincing

   C. friendly

   D. destructive

4. The author suggests that the winner of the battle will be

    A. the vigilant

    B. the active

    C. the brave

    D. all of the above*


5. The word in the selection that means opponent or enemy is

    A. adversary*

    B. supinely

    C. vigilant

    D. forged


6. Which word in line #11 means watchful and careful?

    A. brave

    B. active

    C. vigilant*

    D. strong


7. Patrick Henry's call to action is

    A. "Shall we gather strength by irresolution and inaction?"

    B. " . . . sir, we shall not fight our battles alone."

    C. "The war is inevitable and let it come!"*

    D. "They tell us, sir, that we are weak . . . "

# Bibliography

Adams, Marilyn Jager. "The Challenge of Advanced Texts: The Interdependence of Reading and Learning," in *Reading More, Reading Better: Are American Students Reading Enough of the Right Stuff?* New York: Guildford Publications, 2009, 163-189.

ACT, *Reading Between the Lines: What the ACT Reveals About College Readiness in Reading*, accessed November 27, 2011. http://www.act.org/research/policymakers/reports/reading.html.

Aurelius, Marcus, trans. George Long. *The Thoughts of the Emperor Marcus Aurelius Antoninus.* London: George Bell & Sons, 1890.

Betts, E. A. *Foundations of Reading Instruction, with Emphasis on Differentiated Guidance.* New York: American Book Company, 1946.

California Invasive Plant Council, "Invasive Plant Inventory," accessed November 27, 2011. http://www.cal-ipc.org/ip/inventory/index.php.

Common Core State Standards Initiative, "The Standards," accessed November 27, 2011. http://www.corestandards.org/the-standards.

Dickinson, Emily. Poets.org, "A Bird Came Down the Walk," accessed November 27, 2011. http://www.poets.org/viewmedia.php/prmMID/20949.

Dickinson, Emily. Cuny.edu, "Hope." Last modified February 25, 2009, accessed November 27, 2011. http://academic.brooklyn.cuny.edu/english/melani/cs6/hope.html.

Donne, John. "For whom the bell tolls a poem (No man is an island)," accessed November 27, 2011. http://www.poetry-online.org/donne_for_whom_the_bell_tolls.htm.

Douglass, Frederick. *Narrative of the Life of Frederick Douglass an American Slave, Written by Himself.* Boston: Anti-Slave Office, 1845.

Henry, Patrick. Patrick Henry Center for Individual Liberty, "Patrick Henry's Speeches," accessed November 27, 2011. http://www.patrickhenrycenter.com/Speeches.aspx.

Hu Hsueh-chao, Marcella, and Paul Nation. "Unknown Vocabulary Density and Reading Comprehension," in *Reading in Foreign Language 13*, no. 1 , 2000. 403-430.

Laufer, Batia. "What Percentage of Text-Lexis is Essential for Comprehension?" in *Special Language: From Humans Thinking to Thinking Machines*. Clevedon: Multilingual Matters, 1989, 316-323.

Lillian Goldman Law Library, "Washington's Farewell Address 1796," accessed November 27, 2011. http://avalon.law.yale.edu/18th_century/washing.asp.

Marzano, Robert J., Debra J. Pickering, and Jane E. Pollock. *Classroom Instruction That Works: Research Based-Strategies for Increasing Student Achievement.* Alexandria: ASCD, 2001.

McNamara, Danielle S. *Reading Comprehension Strategies: Theory, Interventions, and Technologies.* Florence: Psychology Press, 2007.

National Aeronautics and Space Administration, "Mars Exploration Program," accessed November 27, 2011. http://mars.jpl.nasa.gov/allaboutmars/extreme.

Office of Superintendent of Public Instruction for state of Washington, "SMARTER Balanced Assessment Consortium," accessed November 27, 2011. http://www.k12.wa.us/smarter.

Paine, Thomas. The Independence Hall Association (ushistory.org), "Common Sense," accessed November 27, 2011. http://www.ushistory.org/paine/commonsense/sense5.htm.

Pearson, David P., Laura R. Roehler, Janice A. Dole, and Gerald G. Duffy. *Developing Expertise in Reading Comprehension.* Newark: International Reading Association, 1999.

Partnership for Assessment of Readiness for College and Careers, "PARCC Model Content Frameworks," accessed November 27, 2011. http://www.parcconline.org/parcc-content-frameworks.

Quindlen, Anna. The Daily Beast, "A Quilt of a Country," accessed January 1, 2012.
http://www.thedailybeast.com/newsweek/2001/09/27/a-quilt-of-a-country.html.

SMARTER Balanced Assessment Consortium Staff, Work Group Members, and Technical Advisory
Committee "APPENDICES D–F: Provided in Conjunction with Content Specifications with
Content Mapping for the Summative Assessment of the Common Core State Standards for
English Language Arts & Literacy in History/Social Studies, Science, and Technical Subjects"
accessed November 27, 2011. http://www.k12.wa.us/SMARTER/ContentSpecs/ELA-LiteracyC
ontentSpecificationsAppend.pdf.

The Independence Hall Association, "Constitution of the United States," accessed November 27, 2011.
http://www.ushistory.org/documents/constitution.htm.

Twain, Mark. Yankeeweb.com, "Huckleberry Finn," accessed November 27, 2011.
http://www.yankeeweb.com/library/twain/huck/huck_5.html.

**Notes:**

**Notes:**

**Notes:**